FRED ROSS

CONQUERING GOLIATH

CESAR CHAVEZ AT THE BEGINNING

Foreword by Senator Edward M. Kennedy

An El Taller Grafico Press Book
United Farm Workers/ Keene, California

 163

An El Taller Grafico Press Book

First edition

Distributed by:
El Taller Grafico
P.O. Box 62, La Paz
Keene, California 93531
Tel. (805) 822-5571

Copy Editor: Marc Grossman
Front cover design: Andrea Duflon
Front cover photo of Cesar Chavez: George Ballis
Other photos: Victor Aleman

Library of Congress Catalog Card Number
89-52079
ISBN 0-9625298-0-X

Printed and bound in the United States of America

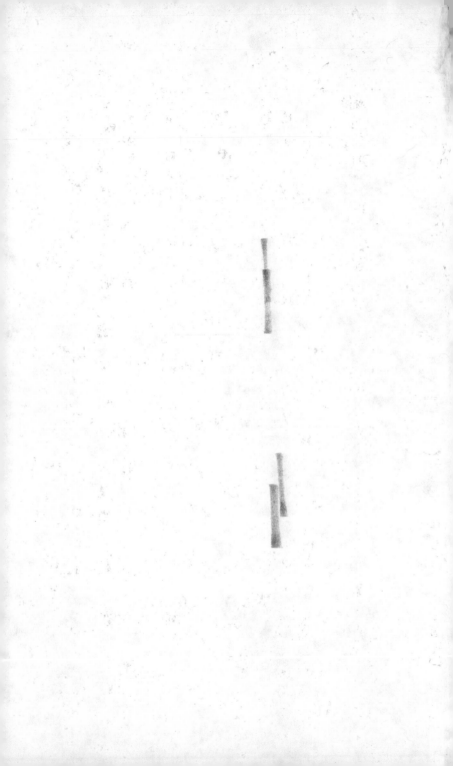

Oh, the foes will rise with the sleep still in their eyes,
And they'll jerk from their beds and think they're dreaming.
But they'll pinch themselves and squeel and they'll know
that it's for real, the hour that the ship comes in.
And they'll raise their hands, say 'we'll meet all your demands,'
But we'll shout from the bow, 'your days are numbered.'
And like Pharoah's tribe, they'll be drownded in the tide,
And like Goliath, they'll be conquered.

"When The Ship Comes In"
Bob Dylan

TABLE OF CONTENTS

Foreword

For decades, farm workers were the forgotten labor force of America, struggling for the same rights that other workers took for granted. *The Grapes of Wrath* came and went, but the brutality of the vineyards remained.

Conquering Goliath tells the story of the first successful attempt to organize farm workers. It took place in the seaside farm town of Oxnard, California, and marked the start of the extraordinary career of Cesar Chavez. In three decades, this incredibly dedicated leader has transformed the way farm workers are treated in this country, touched the lives of millions of others, in and out of agriculture, and brought America closer to the ideals of equality and justice.

Robert Kennedy once said that Cesar was "one of the heroic figures of our times," committed to both justice and non-violence with equal passion. The plight of farm labor in America is still of great concern, but Cesar Chavez and the United Farm Workers, using its tools of non-violence— the marches, the masses, the protests, the strikes, and the boycott—have ensured that their cause will not be ignored.

Conquering Goliath is the story of Cesar Chavez' first battles to organize California farm workers. It is also a primer on community organization and social and political change. Saul Alinsky's admonition of the need to convert one person at a time, time after time, until victory is achieved is evident in the grass-roots strategy that Cesar developed. Also apparent is the underlying belief that societies must be transformed from within by mobilizing individuals and communities.

It is not surprising that Cesar's words come through with such clarity in these pages, since they were recorded by Fred Ross, his teacher and mentor. They met in 1952 when Cesar was working in apricot orchards outside San Jose, California. Ross' own organizing career stretches back to the Depression. This book vividly transports the reader back to the late 1950's when the very idea of unionizing farm workers was revolutionary.

Rarely do readers feel that they are witnessing the birth of a dynamic social movement. Seldom does a book succeed in telling how history was made, while enabling readers to listen to the thoughts, fears, and hopes of those who made that history. *Conquering Goliath* does that, and more.

It also recounts a sordid, though largely ignored, period of history when several hundred thousand Mexican laborers—braceros, they were called—were imported to work on American farms. The influx began during the Second World War, when growers claimed that the war effort had produced a shortage of field workers to cultivate and harvest the crops. But after the war, the braceros kept coming. Growers argued that their fruits and vegetables would wither and die if the stream of braceros was halted.

The program was supposed to give domestic workers the first opportunity for farm jobs, and protect imported braceros from abuse. But the law was largely ignored by growers, and it was rarely enforced by the Department of Labor or by the state employment services administering the program until it was repealed by Congress.

In California, domestic farm workers suffered from severely depressed wages, poor working conditions, and frequent unemployment. The 1965 Delano Grape Strike, led by Cesar Chavez, protested wages of 85 cents an hour for vineyard workers—the consequence of two decades of depressed pay caused by the bracero program.

The braceros fared just as poorly. They endured long hours of back-breaking work, miserable working conditions, wretched food, and housing in overcrowded, barracks-like labor camps. Much of their meager wages were docked to pay for overpriced room and board.

Conquering Goliath is a down-to-earth human drama, a gripping and accurate tale of these events. It is also a lesson in non-violence, and a reminder of how much can be accomplished when a courageous individual stands up against injustice. Viva la Causa.

Edward M. Kennedy
United States Senator

Washington, D.C.

Chapter 1

The Helstein Plan

The way it happened, at about ten o'clock that night in the fall of 1958, I walked into the C.S.O. office in Oxnard, and there was Cesar coming toward me. "Let's go someplace where we can talk," he said, moving on without slowing through the door and out to my car in front. We crossed the tracks and drove down Oxnard's main drag to the Kewpie Doll Cafe.

"Stop here," he said. "We can sit in the car and gab."

I parked just out of the line of traffic, got my tape recorder ready, and gave him a quick once-over. In the four months since I had seen him, he had withered away to practically nothing but the glazed eyes sunk deep in the dark Indian face, darker than ever now where the smudge from only four hours' sleep a night was pushing down from the eyes in purple patches.

"Christ, Cesar!" I said. "If you don't watch it—" But he was already letting it go, the words tumbling out so fast that, what with the blatting horns and groaning trucks and general traffic commotion on the drag, I could hardly take them in. For over four hours the stream of words kept coming, shot through with the pure hell of the first four months of his apprenticeship to the farm workers who lived in the little seaside town of Oxnard, fifty miles north of Los Angeles.

"Of course, Fred," he sighed, "I'd always been wild to get into it. All through the years with you and the C.S.O. Even way back to that first night and the meeting at my place in San Jose. Remember?"

Remember? As though it had been caught and chiseled forever somewhere deep in my retina, it was suddenly there again: the tiny, narrow house on Scharf Street with the proud little gate, Cesar's wife, Helen, opening the door.

In the late spring of 1952, I had come to San Jose to build a chapter of the Community Service Organization. The C.S.O., as we called it, was a civil rights-civic action movement among the Chicanos with, at that time, the reputation of being the most militant and effective organization of its kind in the United States. I had just completed the organization of the mother-chapter in East L.A., and was bringing word of its wonders to the

East Side of San Jose and to the home, that night, of a young man named Cesar Chavez.

But I was about the last guy Cesar Chavez wanted to meet in the tough eastside San Jose barrio they nicknamed "Sal Si Puedes" (which translates "get out if you can"). It was where Cesar and his family often called home since they began life as migrant farm workers in the late 1930's. Cesar was ten when the bank foreclosed on the small family farm his grandfather had homesteaded during the late 1880's in the Gila River Valley outside Yuma, Arizona.

Many of the people who lived in Sal Si Puedes worked in the orchards and vineyards which then flourished outside of town. It seemed that the only way young men left Sal Si Puedes was to go off to jail, the military or the cemetery. Cesar was then laboring in apricot orchards outside San Jose, where he had come to settle after getting out of the Navy at the end of the war.

Cesar had found out, years before, that whenever a gringo wanted to meet you, look out! In those days, Sal Si Puedes was right in the path of a stream of college people coming down from Berkeley and Stanford to write their theses about the barrio. They would ask insulting questions like "How come the Mexican Americans have so many kids? And how come they all eat beans and chile?" Then they would all go back and become professors and teach their students how to go down to the barrio and write their theses.

So Cesar thought I was one of them, he told me later. Except he wasn't completely sure about it because I had this old beat-up car and wore wrinkled clothes.

Anyway, because of the history, he didn't want to meet with me at first. Whenever I'd come by, when Helen said Cesar would be home, he just wouldn't be there. But this didn't work because I kept coming back. So finally, he gave in and we met.

But he hadn't quit trying to "organize" against me. He hatched a plan with his Pachuco buddies to scare me away from the "housemeeting" Cesar had agreed to hold with his friends in the neighborhood. At a certain point during the meeting, he would switch his cigarette from one hand to the other, and that would be the signal for them to start insulting me. Then, he thought, I would leave and they would get "even."

He watched me get out of that old beat-up jalopy of mine and walk to the porch. Helen opened the door and I entered a tiny living room. On each side of the room were old, broken-down couches loaded with guests. In the kitchen, grownups were looking over each other's shoulders, and little kids were peeking out between the legs.

I came on in, between couches and knees, shaking hands along the way. When I put my hand toward Cesar, instead of getting up, he just sort of rocked forward on his behind, and raised it an inch or two off the couch. When he shook my hand, it felt like a small piece of pig's liver. I got the same kind of non-welcome from the others, too.

After sitting down, I took out a cigarette and held out the pack. No takers. I thought, hm, no smokers. So I started smoking and, right away, the packs came out all around the room. Everybody was smoking; they just weren't smoking mine.

So then we started the housemeeting. I told Cesar and his buddies I had worked all over Southern California. And wherever I went the conditions among the Mexican Americans were as bad as in Sal Si Puedes. The same polluted creeks and horse pastures for kids to play in. The same kind of cops beating up young guys and "breaking and entering" without warrants. The same mean streets and walkways, and lack of street lights and traffic signals. The same poor drainage, overflowing cesspools, and amoebic dysentery.

Cesar was impressed. He realized I knew his problems as well as anyone. I didn't rabble-rouse; I just talked quietly about what I had done helping the people of Riverside and Redlands, in the Casa Blanca and El Modena barrios, do away with segregation in the schools and skating rinks and schoolbuses. And how, on the eastside of Los Angeles, the people built their own civic-action organization (the C.S.O.), which went to work on their problems as well as registering neighbors to vote and turning them out to the polls.

I told them about the C.S.O.'s response to "Bloody Christmas 1951," when seven young Chicanos were nearly beaten to death by drunken cops. And how never before, in the whole history of Los Angeles, had any cop ever gotten "canned" for beating up a Mexican American. If the people of Los Angeles could do it, I said, there was no reason why we couldn't do the same sort of thing in Sal Si Puedes, if we wanted to badly enough.

About then, one of Cesar's Pachuco friends got tired of waiting for the signal because all of a sudden he butted in and asked how come I was sticking my big nose in. Cesar had forgotten about his little "plan." So he told the guy in "Calo" (Pachuco language) to either keep his big mouth shut or get out. He shut up.

"You remember?" Cesar said now, huddled there in the half-dark on the passenger side of the front seat of my car on Oxnard's main drag. "I asked if you thought the C.S.O. could ever help the farm workers. 'It sure can,' you said. 'After we get organized. If the people want it.'"

"Well, it took a long time," he said, "but we're finally doing it, I guess."

The day after that meeting at his house, Cesar had come out to head up the first voter registration drive ever held in the barrio. Others fell by the wayside, but Cesar had ploughed right on through for forty consecutive nights, achieving a final total of over four thousand newly registered Chicano voters.

The following year, I convinced my boss, Saul Alinsky, head of the Chicago-based Industrial Areas Foundation (I.A.F.), to hire Cesar. For the next ten years, we worked together, organizing C.S.O. chapters in all of the major barrios in California. We led drives that registered over 500,000 Chicanos to vote, brought U.S. citizenship and old-age pensions to approximately 50,000 Mexican immigrants, fought for installation of paved streets, sidewalks, traffic signals, recreational facilities and clinics, and forced a drastic curb on police brutality and "urban removal" of Spanish-speaking residents from redevelopment projects in many of those same barrios.

Then, one day, the wire from Saul Alinsky came, calling Cesar and me to San Francisco to meet with him, Ralph Helstein, head of the United Packinghouse Workers of America (U.P.W.A.), and Tony Rios, national president of the C.S.O., to discuss the "Helstein Plan."

The Helstein Plan called for the U.P.W.A. to join forces with the C.S.O. in establishing a pilot project which, if successful, could set the ground-work for launching a national farm workers' movement. Oxnard was selected as the starting point because of its heavy Chicano farm worker population and because the union already had a base there in the fruit and vegetable sheds.

This joint union-C.S.O. organizing plan evolved at the height of the bracero farm labor program. The United States government had begun importing bracero farm workers from Mexico to work mostly in Southwest agriculture because of alleged labor shortages brought on by World War II. But growers liked the compliant and underpaid braceros so much that they managed to extend the program after the war ended, even though the labor shortage had passed. During the 1950's and early '60's, hundreds of thousands of foreign field laborers were imported to work on U.S. farms, including the citrus- and vegetable-growing region around Oxnard.

The pilot project was to be a sort of hybrid C.S.O. It would encompass the usual functions of an ordinary C.S.O. chapter, but its major concern would be with the farm workers through development of a Farm Worker Employment Committee, infinitely stronger and more effective than those in any of the other chapters.

At the "appropriate point" in its history (presumably when sufficient "union consciousness" had been developed among its members), this committee would sever its connection with its mother-C.S.O. and attach itself to a new "host," the union.

Of not inconsiderable importance to the C.S.O., which was then struggling to obtain financial self-sufficiency, was the promise that the United Packinghouse Workers would sweeten the pot to the tune of twenty thousand dollars, provided Cesar agreed to do the job.

"Jesus! Fred," Cesar exclaimed, "I didn't let on but I didn't know what in hell to say when they offered me that job. In one way, I was gung-ho to do it. But at the same time, there was this fear thing—like, maybe I'm asking for too much, and what if I fail—that kept creeping in. You know how it is. Over the years you hear those little things about how good you are. Of course, you don't believe them at first. But they sound good. So after a while you start believing them a little bit. Well, quite a bit, I guess.

"So, what have you got? A reputation, and naturally you want to hold onto it. Then one day, zingo! Up comes this deal with the farm workers—the only ones they've never been able to organize—and all of a sudden you've got to take that little bit of fame and lay the whole thing out there on the line. It's a pretty scary thing, Fred.

"But what the hell can you do? You've got to go on living with yourself, you know. Besides, if you don't try you'll never know. You'll go through life thinking, 'Maybe I could have done it after all!' Well, you know the rest, Fred."

Cesar had finally taken the job. Then, at the insistence of the C.S.O. board, he and Helen and the seven kids had gone to Carpenteria State Beach ten miles north of Oxnard so he could get a little rest before beginning the work.

Chapter 2

Hunting for the Key

Cesar had tried to relax, but every time he started to let go, the thought of that twenty thousand dollars, along with the nebulous dimensions of the new job, had tightened him up again. He had always been paid, of course, while he was working with me and Alinsky. But there the salary, such as it was, had come from the rich. Now it would come directly from the workers. And that was different.

"See, Fred," he said, "I was deathly afraid I would take that money and not use it right. Because getting money from the union, you let your imagination free-wheel back to the early beginnings of the Packinghouse Workers and how they slaughtered the pigs and cows on this real hard, messy job. You sorta see this big mass of people, Red and White and Black and Brown, all reaching into their pockets and pulling out their pennies and nickels and dimes. And finally, making up this huge pot of twenty thousand dollars and sending it out to me to do the job with.

"That was another thing: what the hell was the job? That's what keeps eating on me while I'm sitting there with Helen on this long white bench next to this little camp that this bunch of Cub Scouts were setting up. The guy in charge has the whole thing organized: troop unloads, sets up tents, goes swimming, eats, builds campfire, goes to bed.

"Gee, Fred!" he said, "watching all this, I keep wishing so hard that someone would come along and give me the 'Key' to this whole damned thing I'm saddled with. One of those great organizing plans: Roman Numeral I and then Capital A, that sort of thing. Something to tell me how I'm going to get to the farm workers, for one thing. But also to show me what this line is that I'm supposed to go up to, and then stop and turn the whole thing over to the union."

The more he had thought about it the more charged up he got, until finally, on the pretext of looking for a place to rent in Oxnard, he slammed out of there and went into the little town to see if, maybe, somehow, just being with the people would help him find the "Key."

The Colonia hadn't changed much since he was there as a migrant kid tying carrots with the family twenty years before. There was Juanita

School, where the kids used to bug him every day for wearing the same old clothes—the only ones he had. The old shack was still there, where they had pitched the tent the day they first landed in town. It had been raining that night, he had recalled, and he and his brother, Richard, had reached out through a hole in the tent and caught the rain in their hands.

But some things had changed. On the western edge of the Colonia, blocking what had once been the main entrance and exit way, was a huge sugar factory. He had heard how they had tricked the Chicanos into voting for it by telling them an underpass would be put in as soon as they got the factory built. That had been five years ago, and still no underpass. Without it, a Colonia home could burn to the ground before the firetruck reached the scene from the firehouse across town.

"Then I saw them, Fred, sort of a two-way trickle along the edge of town. Like ants, only they were men, farm workers imported from Mexico: braceros. I followed the braceros from Oxnard's main drag out to where they went through this high steel fence, near a grove of eucalyptus trees. There, inside of the gate, I could see the camp. I'd heard about it being the biggest bracero camp in the United States, but I never dreamed it would be so big! First, they had this building marked "Administration." Then this huge mess-hall. And behind that, these rows and rows of barracks as far as you could see that housed over four thousand workers. The whole thing painted an off-babyshit brown and yellow.

"Across the entrance there was this sign:

Buena Vista Camp

Ventura County Farm Labor Association"

From there, Cesar had gone over to check the action at the United Packinghouse Workers Union. Their office was a storefront on the bottom floor of an old, two-story building. Upstairs was a chop suey joint and next door a drive-in they called the Blue Onion.

The office was in two parts. In the back was a small, partitioned-off space where a woman was typing and a man was working a mimeograph machine. The front was empty except for four or five rows of folding chairs.

"So I go in there, Fred," he said, "and stand by one of the chairs watching them. The woman looks up and keeps right on typing. Pretty quick the guy slows up the mimeo crank and turns to me: 'What can we do for you?' he wants to know.

keeps drinking his beer. So I ask him again.

"This time he puts his beer down and folds his hands on the counter. 'You bein' serious?' he asks me, 'or just making talk?'

"'No, I really want to know,' I tell him. 'I'm from outa town, and—'

"'Man! You must be!' He shakes his head. 'You wan' to tie carrots?— buck fifty, buck sixty a day?'

"'Hell, no!' I act like I've been insulted. 'I got a family.'

"'Then you better keep movin',' he says. 'That's the only work you going to find around here.'

"He lowers his voice. 'All the good jobs go to these guys from Mexico.' He looks around the room, drains his beer and edges out the door.

"'You really lookin' for work?' a guy on my left wantsa know. He's sort of an Indian-looking guy. Mop of real black hair, you know, and this dark face slanting down from his high, wide cheekbones to his chin.

"'Yeah!' I tell him. 'In a way. You working?'

"'Too old,' he grins. 'I have seventy years.' Then he gets this thoughtful look. ''Course it was hard enough in the old days when I used to work in the lemons. But at least then, there were no braceros around.'

"'Oh,' I told him, 'you used to work in the groves, unh?'

"'Thirty years of it.' The way he says it, you can tell he's pretty proud. 'I've got my badge to prove it,' he says, pulling his shirt away from his neck. Sure enough, on both sides of his shoulders you can see where the straps from the sack have dug deep down into him.

"Christ! I think, with all that experience this old guy could probably give me the real word on this farm worker stuff. 'Course, I figure I know most of it anyway, from seeing it myself, and what I've read in the reports from the LaFollette Senate Committee hearings and the President's Advisory Committee and Public Law 78, and all. But even so, you never know with a guy like this. Maybe he'll help me find this 'Key' I'm hunting for.

"'Yeah,' I sort of sigh. 'I guess you've been studying this bracero thing a long time, unh?'

"'Right from the beginning,' he nods. 'When the government brought 'em over for the growers during the War. Of course, they needed 'em then because the "locals" were all in the Service. That's when they found out that this of the braceros was a thing of great riches. So after the War, when there were plenty of "locals" again, they just could not bring themselves to part with the braceros.'

"'How do you mean?' I'm still playing dumb.

"'Dinero, hombre.' He rubs his thumb against his index finger. 'Puro dinero! First place, the grower has little expense of recruitment; the government brings them practically to his gate. He gouges them on wages. He works them twelve to fifteen hours a day, on Saturday and Sunday and holidays. If they complain, or join a union, or do anything but work their ass off, pfft! He slams them back to Mexico!

"'But that's only part of it,' he said. 'The grower charges them a dollar seventy-five a day for slop worth half that much. When there's no more work, he shoots 'em back to the border, so there's no welfare load on him. Hombre!' he throws up his hands. 'How can you expect the "local" to compete with such a thing as this?'

"'It's true,' I nod and nudge him just a little bit more. 'But what's the answer?'

"'Huh!' He turns from me toward the window over the bar. 'No problem there. Ship 'em all back to Mexico and keep 'em there!'

"'Ojalá!' I nod, "that it could be! But between now and then?'

"'Quien sabe,' he sorta shrugs, 'who knows?'

"I decide to quit farting around. 'You—uh, well—do you think any of 'em might want to do something about it? The "locals," I mean.'

"'Como no?' He gives this short laugh. 'How could it be otherwise?'

"Now I figure I'll test him on this 'powerful grower' shit! 'You think they'd be willing to stand up for their rights—even if it means fighting the Association?'

"He raises his head a little and rubs his chin. Then he makes these quick nods. 'I think so—providing they think there's any chance at all that— Say,' he gives me this crinkly-eyed look—'who are you?'

"After we've introduced ourselves and I've held this sort of impromptu meeting with him about C.S.O., I figure I've found a 'live' one in Señor Garcia, so I ask him: 'You think you could take me around to see some of the old-time lemon pickers?'

"'I think so,' he says.

"'When?' I push him. 'Right now?' I'm itching to get moving.

"He looks at the clock above the bar. 'It's pretty late. Besides, there's no hurry—they'll still be there.'

"'How do you mean?' I ask.

"He gives me this real sort of serious look. 'Most of 'em are down there in the cemetery, and—' I guess my smile looks pretty sad because, while he's sliding down off the barstool, he puts his hand on my shoulder: 'Don't worry, Señor Chavez, we're not all underground yet. You be at my house tomorrow morning and we'll find plenty of 'em for you to talk to, unh?' He gives me this sorta solemn wink, and leaves.

"By the time I get back to Carpenteria, Helen's out in front of the tent waiting for me. I tell her what happened and how I forgot all about looking for that house to rent. She's hurt, but she takes it pretty well. 'You know, Cesar,' she says, 'there's just something in you about working. You just can't seem to stay still.'

"'But, Helen,' I tell her. 'If you only knew what's happening to me. There's something tearing me inside. All this excitement and expectation! I just want to get started—right now! And yet, at the same time, I don't want to,' I said, taking her hand.

"Anyway, Fred, this went on for a couple of days, and I went to Oxnard every afternoon. About the third day, I forgot to go home for dinner. I just completely forgot!

"'You might as well go then,' says Helen. 'Even if you stay here with us, you're not going to be really here.'

"I just sit there, quiet, listening to the waves. After a while, we go to bed.

"It's quite a while before I can conk off, though. I keep wondering what this thing is we are going to do with the farm workers that will mean so much it will just kind of draw them into C.S.O. like a magnet. Of course, I know how to help them get any back wages the grower won't pay them. And how to get them Workman's Compensation when they get hurt on the job. But where do we go from there? It's got to be something big they have all got in common. Something that will keep them coming back to C.S.O. for more and more and more. Yeah, but what?

"Then I remembered way back, Fred, to something you told us in the early days in San Jose. C.S.O. was getting pretty well-known in the Colonia, and this made the old-time leaders of other organizations envious; so they started badmouthing us. Remember? So we asked you what we ought to do about it.

"'Ignore them!' you said. 'What's the use of spending a lot of time making plans about things you haven't any control over? Just keep on working towards the things you already know about, like recruiting new members, building your power. Pretty soon you'll be so strong those other guys will want to ally themselves with C.S.O. That'll be the end of the problem.'

"Remembering that, I can see I've got to put everything I've got into building the Oxnard C.S.O. In the course of doing that, the 'Key' will come. Of course, that gets me thinking that instead of lying there in bed, I ought to be back in Oxnard talking to some farm worker. And I drift off to sleep knowing that every day I'm going to be spending more and more time in town, and less and less with the family there at the beach. Until, pretty quick, I won't be here at all. And that will be the end of the vacation."

Chapter 3

The Little-Guy-With-the-Bottle

Next day, Cesar started the "housemeeting" organizing drive. The idea was simply to persuade one person at a time in the Colonia to invite a few friends, relatives, and neighbors to the house to meet with Cesar. This would give him a shot at convincing them, under the most favorable circumstances, to join C.S.O. It was also an ideal way of drawing people out, getting them to discuss things that were bothering them and, in the process, to sell themselves and each other on the value of the organization.

Most important of all was the "crunch." This came at the end of the housemeeting, and was the point at which Cesar had to convince the guests to invite people to their home to meet with him. By never failing to "crunch" people at succeeding housemeetings, Cesar was able to build a solid chain of small meetings, leading, at the end of four or five weeks, to a large, Colonia-wide organizing meeting. At that time, he would call together all of the people he had met at the housemeetings and form the Oxnard C.S.O.

Cesar had begun his drive in the home of Señor Garcia the day after their fortuitous meeting at El Mirador. When he arrived at the house that first morning, the old man had had to gab awhile and work in his garden before he was ready to take Cesar around to meet his buddies. The following morning, it was just a quick cup of coffee and off they went. By the end of the week, when Cesar pulled up in front of the house, Garcia was waiting for him, the garden was in weedy disarray, and Mrs. Garcia was no longer speaking to Cesar.

But, while the old fellow's singlemindedness was a little rough on his family, it had helped to create a kind of instant momentum that sent the good word rippling out all over the Colonia. Hearing what C.S.O. had accomplished in other areas around the state was like a tantalizing foretaste of fantastic feasts to come to Oxnard. People could hardly wait for Cesar to finish the organizing drive so they could bring forth their lifelong accumulations of wrongs for him to right.

"But the one thing I didn't bring up, Fred," he said, "was the farm worker situation. In the first place, it's just not in my pitch, because none of the other C.S.O. chapters that I tell the people about has ever been bothered by it, as you know. And then, of course, when you're up there in front of the people at a housemeeting trying to win them over, piling up all those big things the various chapters have done, getting this power feeling and 'big me,' having the people with you—why bring up something you have no answer for, no 'plan?' Besides, they're not bringing it up either, thank God."

Then one night they did. Cesar was just winding up the housemeeting at the home of old man Mejia, one of the real worker-leaders, when Chavira, a younger worker just up from Brawley, mentioned that he just got a Referral Card from the State Farm Placement Service to work in the carrots. The second he mentioned 'carrots'—one of the most detested words in an Oxnard farm worker's vocabulary—the room was smoking with elaborate curses directed with equal fervor at a man named Zamora, who managed the Ventura Farm Labor Association camp, at some exotic variety of toilet tissue known as 'Referral Card,' and at a person named Bates at the State Farm Placement Service office.

"'What do you mean?' Mejia asks Chavira. 'To tie carrots there is no necessity to have a Referral Card. One goes directly to the field and is hired.' (Fred, I don't know what the hell they're talking about with all of this Referral Card business, and going to the Farm Placement and all. But why let on and show how stupid I am?)

"Anyway, Chavira flips his fingers over his head and says, 'Oh, I know that. I went out to the carrots later on. I got the Referral Card so I could talk to Zamora at the Association about one of those eighty-five cents an hour jobs in the tomato seedlings, or irrigation, or planting.'

"'O-o-o-h!' Mejia sneers. 'What a dreamer! You still hoping that that goat-lover Zamora is going to give you a job someday?'

"'Hey, Mr. Chavez, listen to this,' a guy named Yslas says. 'You know why they won't give me a job? It's because I don't like that kind of work! This is what they say at the Association.' He laughs in resentment. 'Yeah, me and all the rest of us local guys. We're too good to do that job. That's just for the braceros! So they say!

"'Of course I know, and everybody here knows we're the same people. And we used to do those jobs, and bend over and do exactly the same thing. But now, because we're a little older, and because they have the braceros, they have decided we don't like farm work anymore.' He bends his head and makes this sort of clucking sound. Then he looks up real quick: 'Hey, Chavez, you think C.S.O. could help on that?'

"Well, Fred, not being able to get a decent wage is one thing, and I know about that. This thing of not being able to get a job, though, catches me by surprise. 'Course I've got a standard stall for stuff like that:

"'Sure, after we get organized,' I tell him, 'if the people want it—' Exactly the same thing you pulled on me in Sal Si Puedes, Fred, when we first met each other.

"'Forget it, Chavez.' Yslas laughs again like it's a real joke to think the C.S.O. could take on the Association. After that, they get on 'those damned Referral Cards' again and 'those bastards Bates and Zamora,' and, of course, the carrots. Finally we break it up and go home.

"Well, I don't pay too much attention to it that night, Fred, or even after it comes up at some of the other housemeetings. I'm sympathetic but not too interested. For one thing, I figure it's only happening to a few guys, that all the rest are holding down those eighty-five cents an hour jobs. I just don't realize, Fred, how serious the problem is.

"Another thing, I can't see yet how I'll be able to work on this job thing. I'm so damned busy getting the C.S.O. going and working on the problems I know the answers to, and wanting like hell to make a big booming success of it, I just haven't got the time for anything else. Besides, the ones that bring it up are people I've already got hooked on C.S.O. by helping them with some other problem, so I'm not pushed.

"But there's something else, too, Fred: this kind of an almost-fear that I've got about challenging the authority of the growers. It's a very common thing to hear the workers say, 'Oh, you can't touch the growers, they're too powerful!' But the workers have learned this from someone, Fred."

"Who?" I glanced over at him. "The unions?"

"Why, sure," he said. "This is the explanation that the workers get when they go into a strike and lose. The union brass will tell 'em, 'Well, they were just too powerful; but there will come a day—!' You know.

"So, anyway, I had a little of this—this fear, myself. 'Course, I could always crash through it by thinking how rewarding it would be when we won. Still, there was a little of that fear there even so."

"Like the gunman that you talk about?" I asked him. "What's that story, Cesar?"

"Oh, there's this young guy in the movies, you know, wants to make a name for himself, fast. He knows if he starts trying to accumulate a whole slew of notches on his gun it'll take a long time and hardly anybody will ever hear about it. But if he gets *the* Gunman, the *Real* Gunman, *the One and Only* Gunman, it'll be pretty hard, but if he gets him it'll be worth all the struggle, because he will get all the fame.

"Same way with the growers: you'll have your fear and your suffering, but if you get 'em, you know it'll be worth it.

"But, Fred, between my workload and this little fear of mine, I keep putting off the farm worker thing. I figure I'll let it rock along until the United Packinghouse Workers takes on the whole job of organizing the workers. Then *they* can handle it.

"The only trouble, Fred, as the housemeeting drive goes on, this thing of the jobs keeps coming up. Not a lot, and not at all the housemeetings, just enough so that it starts eating at me, making me feel sorta guilty, you know, because I'm not doing anything about it. Then, too, I can tell that my own stall about waiting until after we're organized and all isn't going to hold them forever. Before long, I'm going to have to come up with some kind of a reasonable answer for 'em."

He hadn't had much luck on it until one night at a housemeeting at Felix's place, when he met Enclan, the "little-guy-with-the-bottle." As it happened, Enclan was one of the few "locals" left in the lemons. Cesar had been aching to find out how the little guy had been able to hold onto his job so long. For a while, after the meeting began, Enclan just sat there quietly. Then he began excusing himself and leaving the room for a minute.

At first, when this had only happened every twenty minutes or so, Cesar thought it was simply a case of weak kidneys. But eventually, just when the frequency of the trips was beginning to disrupt the meeting, Enclan stopped making them. He simply settled back, pulled out his bottle, and started drinking right there in the room.

"By then, he's got this verbal diarrhea so bad, Fred, that pretty quick he comes out with just what I'm waiting for."

According to Enclan, there were only three lemon crews of "locals" left in Ventura County. When the growers had brought in the braceros they had given the newcomers the better jobs and the "locals" the harder, lower-pay, "mop-up" operations. Such treatment, along with other miserable working conditions, had finally driven the other "locals" out. But not Enclan and his buddies.

"You know what they did, Fred? They said, 'No, we're gonna work,' and they kept on taking that shit, and kept on working. The only reason they're still together is because they all believe exactly the same way.

"Gee, Fred, as soon as he says that, I start thinking about those job complaints I've been getting at the housemeetings. Enclan has answered some of my questions, but there's still one thing I gotta find out:

"'How do you hold onto those jobs?' I ask him. 'Doesn't the boss ever fire you?'

"'Oh, sure.' He takes a big swig out of his bottle. 'Lotsa times.'

"'So then, what do you do? Raise hell and picket or something?'

"'Oh, my God, no!' He shakes his head real hard. 'We gotta fight this our own way, or we'll lose the jobs for good. See, when they pay us off some night and give our jobs to the braceros, next morning we all show up for work like nothing happened. And every day we keep coming back and talking to the boss about letting us go back to work. I guess he just gets tired seeing us or maybe he's afraid there will be some kind of trouble or something—because, finally, we get those jobs again.'"

When Cesar left that meeting, he was at least as loaded with excitement as Enclan was with booze, and it was a long time before sleep came.

"When the meeting broke up, Fred, I had no idea how we were going to get those jobs, but at least there was this little island of hope: If those lemon pickers could do it all by themselves by hanging in there with nothing but guts and stubbornness, why couldn't the other 'locals' do it too, especially if C.S.O. would back them?

"But then I back away from the 'problem' again. How many farm workers, I ask myself, are actually out of work? Oh, there's a few, no doubt of that. But aren't most of them still out there in the fields? Oh, sure, working for a lousy eighty-five cents an hour, but working. So the real problem must be wages. But that is something for the United Packinghouse Workers to worry about later on. This thing of the jobs, well, I would just have to push it out of my head."

Chapter 4

Victory at the Polls

———————

Next day, the job worry was there, of course, but Cesar had less time to think about it because of the press of other matters. First, there had been the problem of finding a full-time helper, a slot finally filled by Big John Soria—the giant who worked at the mental hospital—not because he had a lot of experience organizing, but because he was the only one who could take the job!

Next, there had been the job of putting together the C.S.O. Organizing Meeting. This meant revisiting the three hundred some-odd people he had met at seventy-five housemeetings, sending them reminder calls, and making last-minute "just to make sure" phone calls to all of them the night before the meeting. Over two hundred and fifty people had shown up to form the Oxnard C.S.O., install Tony Del Buono, the nurseryman, as president, and show the Oxnard establishment that the Colonia was beginning to get itself together.

Immediately following that meeting, Cesar began the work of encouraging the Colonia's large immigrant population to study for U.S. citizenship. To get this underway, he had to prepare lesson plans, prevail upon the school board to set up night classes, upon instructors to teach them free, upon the elderly population to attend them. Over four hundred people completed the first round of classes and went on to attain United States citizenship.

With the bulk of the alien first generation studying to become citizens, Cesar's next task was to persuade the C.S.O. to convince the largely non-registered non-voting citizen population to become registered voters. Once the C.S.O. leaders had registered these people, they could approach the politicians as the official spokesmen for a powerful new constituency, which they could use as a club over the heads of those politicians.

This was a great idea. The only problem was that a sizable segment of those eligible to register (in Oxnard, as elsewhere in the state) were opposed to the whole concept of voting. Some of them were former voters with long, bitter memories of sleazy public officials who had bought their votes with beer and promises and promptly "sold them down the river" after the election, leaving them sunk in disgust and humiliation. The rest, lacking parental examples and formal education, simply did not understand the voting process.

In light of these factors, the national C.S.O. had, years before, developed an education program for the unregistered. It was implemented by C.S.O. deputy registrars in the semi-dark doorways and porches of literally tens of thousands of Colonia homes all over California in the following manner:

> Hello, I'm from the C.S.O..
>
> We're out here registering everyone in the neighborhood to vote. It only takes three minutes and it's free. By registering, you can do a lot to help our people move forward.
>
> See, when you register, your name goes down on a list of Colonia voters at the Courthouse. The longer that list is, the more pressure we will be able to put on the politicians to get what we need in the Colonia. By registering, you will help us get those chuck-holed roads fixed up. You will help us get more streetlights so the women won't be afraid to step out of the house at night. More traffic signals so that our kids won't get run over so often. Fair treatment of our people by the cops and the District Attorney, the Welfare, Social Security and Immigration. Jobs for the unemployed farm workers. How about it, wouldn't you like to register? Great! Maybe we'd better go inside the house where it's light.

It worked. In the years when the C.S.O. Movement was sweeping northward up the state, the people cooperated "con animo" (with enthusiasm); and C.S.O. deputies registered over three hundred thousand of them to vote. Cesar pushed the same program in Oxnard in 1958-1959, and the people of the Colonia registered in overwhelming numbers.

But getting the people to sign their names on a registration form was one thing; persuading them to go down to the polls and into a mysterious little cubicle behind a curtain was "harina de otra costal" (flour from an entirely different sack). To overcome this difficulty, C.S.O. had long since launched what amounted to "Get Out the Vote Drives," as door-knocking block workers explained the organization's "Philosophy of the Vote," as summed up in the paradox: "By not voting, you can actually vote!"

"If you don't want to vote for any of those guys," the block workers would tell the people, "you don't have to. Just go to the polls, write your name in the signup book and they will give you your voting paper—your ballot. Take that ballot to the little booth behind the curtain, stay there a minute or two, then bring the ballot out and put it in the box—the ballot box.

"Probably you think you won't be voting when you do that. But you will be, even though you don't put a single mark on that paper. You'll be voting for the Colonia, for yourself, for the future of your kids.

"Because see, when you sign that book, that is proof that you went to the polls on Election Day. So your name stays on that list of Colonia voters at the Courthouse; and you help us hold onto the power we built when we registered all of the people to vote. Power to pressure the politicians into making things better out here.

"But look what happens if you don't go to the polls. You will figure you are not voting, right? Oh, you'll be voting all right—*against* the Colonia, *against* yourself, *against* the future of your kids. Because see, when you don't show up at the polls, they cross your name off the list at the Courthouse. Which makes the list that much shorter. Which means we'll have that much less power to put the pressure on those politicians to help us get the things we need to make the Colonia a better place to live in.

"And don't forget, once we lose that power, the only way we're going to get it back will be when someone goes around registering the people again, which probably won't happen until about four years from now. And that's a long time to wait for a better Colonia."

That's the kind of drive that Cesar had set rolling in the Oxnard Colonia three weeks before the November election in 1958. He and John Soria had found someone in each of the fifty blocks who agreed to "Get Out the Non-Voters" by personal visit, by leaflet, by letter and by phone. This was supplemented by Spanish-language radio spots and a daily PA barrage from a squawk-box on Cesar's car enjoining the people not to forget to go out and vote for the Colonia.

Election Day was one pulling, tearing, twelve-hour rush. Five Precinct Captains made hourly checks of those who had voted, raced around to remove those names from the phone lists of their fifty block workers, and turned in the results to C.S.O. headquarters for analysis.

In no time, there was a contest growing. Captains prodded block workers who pled with non-voters in a desperate last-ditch duel to push their respective precincts out in front. Whenever one of these slipped noticeably behind, out went a flying squad of volunteers to concentrate their fire on the recalcitrants. Should anyone manage to resist the appeal of all three field units, that person would soon be besieged by a rash of calls from phoners back at headquarters.

Twelve noon came and went, but nobody stopped for lunch. By two p.m., though, a mass walkout for food was averted only when some of the farm worker women threw themselves in front of the door while others made tacos and coffee on the spot and ministered to the starving.

By five p.m., with only two hours to go, the famished block workers, on the promise of tacos and coffee later, decided to pass up dinner and "ram it" down to the wire. At six p.m., with the polls closing in an hour and over two hundred people who had still failed to vote, the entire crew went into a good-natured but firm tug-of-war and literally dragged the remaining holdouts down to the polls.

"Then it's all over, Fred," Cesar said. "The Captains check the total votes in their precincts and we all go back to the Hut for our tacos and coffee. While they are being prepared, one of the farm workers leads us in singing some of the old-time corridos from the time of the Mexican Revolution; and I make them a little speech:

"'You may not think you accomplished very much,' I tell them, 'but what you did today is something no one has ever done before in the whole history of the Oxnard Colonia. Except for one old lady who was in the hospital, an old man who had died, and some people who had moved or weren't home, you got every single registered voter in the Colonia down behind that little curtain for a total turnout of eleven hundred and six voters. Nearly three times as many as had ever voted before.

"'With that victory at the polls, you've finally talked to the politicians in the only language those guys can understand. In the past, we have talked to them in English and we have talked to them in Spanish, and they didn't know what the devil we were talking about. Why? Because the only language they can understand is the "voting language." So that's the language we'll be using from now on when we go after them for help on your problems. We've got to start doing that right away, too. Otherwise they will think we came after their votes and then sold them down the river, like the politicians have been doing all those years.'

"We get the community reaction fast, Fred. Until then, the local papers had never given us more than a two- or three-inch squib on page ten. After that 'turnout,' we not only got a front-page story but a very—what's the word?—revealing editorial, commending C.S.O. and then, check this, as much as saying they hope that the C.S.O. won't get carried away with their achievement and become irresponsible, power-crazed, or corrupt!"

The day following the appearance of the newspaper editorial, Cesar opened up the doors of C.S.O.'s most honored program, the Service Center, and went to work on a welter of problems that had dogged the workers' days for generations.

While most of these problems were rooted in economic exploitation, more often than not they showed themselves in official discrimination and neglect. Police violence was common, along with deportation, eviction, and denial of a host of social welfare benefits to which the people were clearly entitled. Grower-controlled politicians, responsible for Colonia upkeep, allowed schools, playgrounds, streets and alleys to go to pot, failed to install badly needed streetlights and traffic signals and, in general, turned their back while the Colonia deteriorated and its residents became demoralized and bitter.

Such inequities had rarely been challenged. People, as individuals, had not been able to deal with them; they lacked the know-how and the backing. They had not been able to hire lawyers to do it, or one of the local "coyotes" (notaries public): they were too poor. They had not been able to put the arm on the local politicians for the reasons already mentioned.

But all that had changed now. Cesar could provide the know-how, the C.S.O. the backing, and the voter registration and spectacular turnout at the polls the political clout. The timing had been exactly right for the opening of the Service Center.

"Well, Fred, my helper, old man Garcia, the retired lemon picker I met that first night at the bar, hardly gets the Service Center door open when in pour the people. Some of their problems are routine immigration and welfare cases; but there's a lot of very personal stuff. The sort of thing usually handled by a lawyer or a priest.

"For instance, here's this woman with a kidnap case. She is trying to locate her ex-husband and make him bring back the son he took with him when he walked out on her ten years before. On the off chance, we notified all 32 C.S.O. chapters, and damned if we didn't locate the guy and the kid. No one else had ever offered to help on this, so of course she thinks a lot of C.S.O.

"Then there's this Mrs. Avila, who marries this guy from Mexico and helps him get his permanent visa in this country. Later, both of them help her cousin get her visa. Still later, her husband runs off with the cousin. Mrs. Avila wants to turn both of them over to the Immigration Service and get them deported. We have a long talk, and she agrees to try to forgive and forget.

"Another woman, Mrs. Ida Sanders, comes in about her husband and herself. He's sick and needs some kind of benefits. They never compensated her for an automobile accident she was in. On top of that, her boss fires her because he thinks she's too involved with C.S.O.

"Mrs. Sanders and I start the desk-pounding operation. The State Department of Employment gives Mr. Sanders his Disability Insurance. We get Mrs. Sander's settlement by pressuring the Claims Department of the insurance company and the State Insurance Commission. I think we could have gotten her job back for her too, but after what happened she doesn't want it.

"Then there's Mr. Polanco, who lent his friend some money. The friend won't pay him back, so Mr. Polanco wants to take him to court. We explain to the friend about C.S.O.'s interest in the case, and he pays Polanco the three hundred dollars he's owed him for over three years.

"Here's another guy, Guzman, charged with molesting a child. According to old man Garcia, some nine-year-old girl is playing around on some equipment at the place where he works. It's dangerous, but she won't quit so he sort of jerks her off the machinery. All the men who work with Garcia and his boss attest to this. Garcia claims the mother is upset and is seeking revenge by falsely accusing Guzman of molesting the child.

"The Assistant D.A. has told Garcia and his boss that unless they can come up with some very strong character witnesses, the case will have to go to trial. The only one Garcia knows is his minister, who tells him he can't do it because 'it might set a precedent.' (I can see his point. Christ should have never started feeding the poor. Look at the mess that got us into!)

"The next day, we get a real break. That editorial I told you about on our great turnout at the polls comes out in the afternoon edition of the paper. As soon as I get it, we visit the D.A., and Guzman presents his case and shows him a copy of the editorial. A few days later, the charges against Guzman are dropped.

"Then there's a guy who got 'canned' over a can! Juan Solis is old and forgetful. He forgets to punch his card when he goes to work. Or he might punch it twice and then forget to punch it when he leaves.

"Juan is forgetful once too often. One day, buying his groceries, he absentmindedly puts a can of tuna in his pocket and forgets to give it to the checker at the counter. Juan has worked for the same employer for twenty years and has never stolen from him. He has lived in Oxnard for over fifty years and has never been in jail.

"But the day Juan takes the tuna, he's in jail. Even though the usual procedure on the first offense is to put people on probation.

"Sad to say, since Juan had already stood trial when we found out about his case, the best we could do was to have his sentence reduced from fifteen days to twelve.

"Those are just some of the cases that come to mind, Fred. There's hundreds more just like them."

But the Service Center, with Cesar in command, was much more than your routine problem clinic; it was a sovereign restorative of human dignity and a means of drawing the people ever more deeply into the C.S.O. Meek, self-effacing people, whose lifestyle had been one of being pushed around by the authorities without a peep, soon learned to stand their ground, speak out, and get what they came after. In the agony of forcing themselves to do this, they suffered a sea change: they got organized.

Through the Center, people also learned to "give" themselves to the C.S.O. Most made small contributions—a bag of beans or rice for C.S.O. fundraisers, clothes for the rummage sale, a bit of cash for office supplies. In giving of themselves, Oxnard C.S.O. members moved from mere momentary gratitude for the help they had received to a sense of fierce possessiveness that only comes when people give to others that of which they have so pitifully little themselves.

"Some came begging, Fred, on their own for the chance to give, like old man Campos did. Campos has always worked in the fields. He has small hands, but they are calloused thick clear to the ends of the fingers. On the other side, they are wrinkled and withered and the veins stand out like strips of purple tubing.

"In the early days, Campos was the leader of the Colonia. The people used to turn to him for advice on the patriotic holidays. The lesser leaders looked up to him at the meetings of the lodges and burial societies. In addressing him, they used the title of respect 'Don' before his Christian name.

"But all that is in the past. Over the years, civic and political clubs run by American-born younger people had elbowed the old-time clubs and Campos out of the way. Then along comes the C.S.O. and, in the process of organizing it, we unintentionally left out Campos.

"So now Campos is old and left out, and when he begins to talk about the citizenship classes he is immediately angry. The C.S.O., he says, has no business turning the people against their own country by making them citizens of this one. Many people, he says, are critical of C.S.O. for doing this.

"I'm courteous, Fred, but firm with the old man. 'C.S.O.,' I tell him, 'is not worried about what some of the people are saying, so long as we are giving the majority the programs that they want. If some of the people who are criticizing the C.S.O. would come to the meetings and make their objections known, it would be a good thing, because then they would learn the truth of the old dicho: 'No es lo mismo comer que tirarse con los platos' (It is not the same to stand on the sidelines and criticize as to get into the heat of the battle.)

"At this point, Fred, Señor Campos suddenly changes his tune and offers to help the C.S.O. He also signs up for the citizenship classes, pays his three dollars and fifty cents dues, and becomes a C.S.O. member.

"On the surface, Fred, it looks like Campos has made his fight and lost, but maybe not. Maybe it wasn't the citizenship that brought him to the Service Center at all. It may have been simply that being overlooked by C.S.O. as one of the leaders had cut him. Maybe, underneath he had come in to fight and lose as a way of no longer being overlooked. In losing, he might have won. In giving, he received.

"But everyone gives, Fred. Some when they come to the Center, others when they leave, and still others some time in between. People too poor to contribute cash or kind do odd jobs around the Center or run errands. Even when there's nothing at all for them to do, we find ways of keeping them busy doing that.

"To an outsider, it probably seems ridiculous, Fred, the lengths we will go to in hewing to that line. For instance, one day there's this little group of people sitting around gabbling and sort of enjoying their Center. None of them can read or write, so there's hardly anything I can have them do to help us out. But the longer they sit there, the 'antsier' I get thinking what a shame that all this time is going by and none of them is getting any closer to C.S.O.

"Right then I spot this pile of scrap paper on Big John's desk and all at once this thought pings into my head: 'Hey, John,' I call to him. 'Would you mind bringing me that stack of papers on your desk?' He brings it, and I tell him, 'Now look, what I want you to do is to pass it out to all these people sitting around here and have them tear it into two-inch squares.'

"'What for?' He gets a puzzled expression on his face.

"'I'll tell you later.' I don't know myself yet, but then I get this other flash. 'No, wait a minute,' I tell him. 'The reason we need them—we may have a raffle later on and we'll need tickets. Tell them that—and how important it is, and all.'

"John walks off with his well-it's-news-to-me look and passes out the paper. In about an hour, he comes back with this big cardboard box crammed with little bits of paper. 'Where do you want them?' he wants to know.

"I lean away from the guy I am helping and whisper to John, 'Take them out in the back room and dump them in the garbage can!'

"When I say that, he gives me this look like I'm completely nuts or something. I walk him back to the garbage can, explaining why we got to start letting the people know that everyone who comes around the office is there to help. When I'm pretty sure John's got it, I go back and start working again."

Chapter 5

This Thing of the Jobs

———————

"Just as I sit back down, Mejia, that farm worker I told you about who had the housemeeting, walks in. Soon as I see him, all that stuff about 'the jobs' and braceros I haven't had to even think about lately comes back to me, and I motion him over to my desk.

"'No,' he says, 'there's other people waiting. I'll talk to you later. It's not too important.'

"From that, I figure he doesn't have a problem. He's just hooked on C.S.O. and maybe wants to help. So after we've cleared out the office along about eleven p.m., I chew the fat with him for a while and finally ask him, 'Well, what's up, Señor Mejia?'

"'No, it's not important,' he says, 'I just wanted to gossip a little.'

"'What about?' I ask.

"He looks at these real rough hands of his—black around the nails, big callouses, you know. 'It's this thing of the jobs, Señor Chavez. It's a pretty serious problem, you know. About the biggest one we've got in Oxnard.'

"I just give him this little nod, Fred, more in sympathy than anything else, because I don't believe it's really all that serious. 'Yeah,' I tell him. 'I know it's pretty bad. But still, there's a lot of them working, I guess.'

"He looks at me sort of out from under his eyebrows. 'Where do you think most of the people in C.S.O. are working, Señor Chavez?

"He sort of catches me off-guard. 'Well, gee! I don't know. In the fields, I guess.'

"He kinda cocks his head at me like he didn't hear right, maybe. 'Señor Chavez, you remember at the big Organizing Meeting last week, and the citizenship classes on Wednesday, when you asked the people that worked in the fields to raise their hands?'

"I nod. 'And how many,' he asks, 'do you think are working?'

"'I don't know,' I tell him, 'but from all those hands I saw, I guess most of 'em are.'

"He shakes his head and pushes his lower lip up. 'Sure, they raised their hands, because they're all farm workers. But that doesn't mean they've got a job. No.' He shakes his head. 'Hardly any of 'em get more'n two, three days' work a month on a decent job. The rest of the time they're out there in those buck-sixty, two-buck-a-day jobs in the carrots.'

"'But what about all the other workers?' I ask him.

"'What other workers?' he raises his hands. 'It's the same with practically all the "locals" here in Oxnard. Far as that goes, every place in the state where they've got braceros.'

"Right then I get the idea maybe this guy isn't just in here to blow about the other workers. Maybe he's got a problem himself. 'Are you out of a job, Señor Mejia?' I ask him.

"'Como no,' he chuckles. 'Certainly, that's nothing new. But that's not the reason I came to see you. I just thought—'

"'But,' I cut in, 'if you're looking for a job, maybe we can help. I don't know how, but—'

"'No, Señor Chavez.' He raises the palm of his hand like a shield and turns his head away. 'It's not for myself. It's just to get your advice on this whole thing of the jobs.' He laughs, 'If you start trying to help everybody that's out of work, that's all you'll be doing around here.'

"I'm pretty sure the guy's exaggerating, but the thing is, I'm a little on the defensive about it, too. 'That's funny,' I tell him, 'I guess we've had over four hundred people in here the last three weeks, and you're the first one that ever said anything about jobs.'

"'Oh, that's not hard to explain,' he says. 'We all understand the C.S.O. is not for that.'

"This sorta shakes me, Fred. 'What do you mean?' I ask him.

"'Well, we know that C.S.O. is for citizenship and voting, and all this,' he waves his hand around the office. 'Helping people with their troubles.'

"'What makes you think C.S.O. is just for these things?' I ask him.

"'What else?' He shows me the palms of his hands. 'These are the only things you've been telling us about at our houses and at the big Organizing Meeting.'

"When he says that, all at once something pings into my head. Hell! No wonder only a few of them brought it up at the housemeetings or anywhere else! I never said anything about it. So naturally they figured helping 'em get jobs wasn't part of the C.S.O.'s program. Then I start wondering how many of the guys at those meetings are really out of work. Suddenly I'm feeling kinda sick. 'Course I still don't think it's quite as bad as he says. But even if it's only half or a third that bad, it's bad. *Real bad!*

"Anyway, Fred, I explain why I never brought it up was because there were so many other things I had to bring up first. 'But that doesn't mean we're not going to get into it, Señor Mejia. If the people want us to. The only thing, we just haven't found a way to do it yet.'

"He shakes his head. 'No, Señor Chavez, I guess what we need is a union.'

"'Well, sure,' I agree, 'if you had a union, and it was successful, you could get the jobs and the wages, and many other things. But, Señor Mejia,' I leaned toward him. 'You haven't got any union yet. All you got is C.S.O. So maybe the best thing is to try and see how in the hell we can do something to help.'

"He's still shaking his head: 'No, I don't think so, Señor Chavez. We all like what you are doing very much, the voting and citizenship and the office. It's best, I think, for C.S.O. to stay this way. To fight for jobs would give the organization a bad name. Sort of—well, discredit it, you know.'

"You see, Fred, here's another thing. Before C.S.O., the only groups around for people to belong to were these old-time Mexican patriotic societies and fifty-cents-a-month burial insurance groups and social clubs. But these groups never did anything along a controversial line because they were afraid the law, the government, or the growers would smash them if they did. Well, then C.S.O. comes along and they sorta see it the same way. And I always have to straighten 'em out, just like Mejia now:

"'Now wait a second, Señor Mejia,' I raise my finger at him. 'Don't you worry about the C.S.O. Our main purpose here is to help the farm workers. If we don't, we might as well fold up. You see, if we go into this thing of the jobs, even if we lose, C.S.O.'s not going to be discredited. As long as we make a good fight out of it, the people will see we are trying to help them. It's only when we refuse to fight that we'll be discredited.'

"He sits there shaking his head for a moment before he speaks. 'Well, what do you think we ought to do about it then, Señor Chavez?'

"Hell, I don't know what to tell him, Fred. I'm not even sure I know what he really wants. The only thing that keeps going around in my head is what that 'little-guy-with-the-bottle' told me. That, and this plan we made with the U.P.W.A. to set up a sort of Employment Committee in C.S.O. and get the farm workers into it. I mention this to him.

"'Well, but just what does this Committee do?' he wants to know. I tell him the first thing that comes to my mind: 'It helps the workers fight the growers and the labor contractors who refuse to pay 'em their Workman's Compensation or deduct their Social Security. It teaches the workers the value of joining a union. Uhh—!' But then I've run down.

"'Uh-huh,' Mejia nods his head real slow. 'And what else, Señor Chavez?'

"'Well,' I sort of flip my hands up off my knees. 'That's about it, so far.

But if the workers have other problems—like this employment thing, probably the Committee could help on that, too. We just need to know more about it.' I look at him: 'Probably you're just the guy that can tell us.'

"He tries to, and he knows the answers. The only thing, he just can't find the words. What comes out is all full of Referral Cards and Farm Placement, and how some guy named Zamora gives the braceros preference over the local workers. But all that is all tangled up with the old days, and how every morning the growers would pick up the workers (the Daily Pickup) where they waited around their little fires down by the railroad tracks. Or hire 'em right at the ranch gate (Gate Hiring). And how now, there's no more pickup, no more gate hiring—no more job. Period!

"Well, I keep firing questions at him, Fred, trying to find out exactly what happens; but the poor guy is running out of answers. He keeps trying; but finally he stops: 'You know, Señor Chavez.' He leans his head over and gives it a few quick nods. 'I think it would be good for you to talk to los otros condenados,' he says. 'The ones in the same boat with me, you know. They could probably explain it better, so you could get to really know what the things of not getting a job are really like. Hey!' His eyes go wide. 'Maybe we could make that Committee you told me about. The Employment Committee, uh?'

"'Yeah, we could do that. I guess.'

"'When?'

"'Well, I—uh—'

"'Tomorrow night?'

"'Well, sure, I guess.'

"'Okay, I'll bring the others.'

The next night, Cesar met with the workers. There were ten of them, and it was raining so hard on the metal roof of the Hut that they had to yell to hear each other. What he wanted, Cesar told them, was to get a very good picture of just what was going on.

They didn't want that. What they wanted was a bitching session. They took turns bitching. In a dim sort of way, he had expected it. Before they could get down to business, they had to get some of it off their chests. So they bitched, but little of what he wanted came out. Then he suggested they take the problems one at a time and discuss them.

"'Who's going to be first?' I ask them, yelling over the rain. Nobody answers, so I look around the table. 'You mean everything's OK? You've all got nice fat jobs?' Finally this young guy, Chavira, looks around at the others and then at me:

"'No, Chavez.' He puts his head down and sorta frowns. 'It isn't that.

It's, well—sort of a waste of time. We've been telling you the last two months. You know what's wrong.'

"'Well, I guess I know all right,' I tell him. 'I just know more than I understand, I guess. For example, this Referral Card business.' I hardly get it out of my mouth before they start snickering.

"'Ay, Chavez,' says Campos, still chuckling. 'They serve for nothing, believe me. It's been so long since I fooled with them, they've almost left my mind. Only the ones who've come here lately bother with them.' He grins over at Chavira, who's only been here a while from Brawley.

"'But why do they have those Referral Cards?' I ask them.

"'Because the Farm Labor Association wants them,' says Chavira.

"'No,' says Campos. 'It's the Farm Placement and old Hayes that wants them.'

"'But why?' I keep after them.

"'Well,' says Campos, 'it's sort of like those Union Hiring Halls you had to go through in San Francisco in wartime. They give you a piece of paper and you get a job. That's what old Hayes up there at Farm Placement does—gives you a card. The main difference is that down here you don't get a job.' They all burst out laughing again. And I get exactly nowhere on the subject of Referral Cards.

"After they've quieted down, this middle-aged guy, Ledesma, speaks up: 'Look, Chavez, this is what happens. See, there is this Big Labor Contractor, and I don't mean the Mexican Contractors. I mean the Ventura County Farm Labor Association—which is all the growers put together—which built the Buena Vista Camp to take care of all those 5,000 braceros which is run by that good-for-nothing Zamora. OK?' I nod and he goes on.

"'Well, when you get out there to Buena Vista Camp, mostly you don't get a job. Once in a hundred years though, if you are super lucky, they put you in trucks right with the braceros. When you get to working in the fields, the field-boss works the hell out of you. He demands more work out of you than from the braceros, for less money. Then he insults you. Finally, you get so mad and fed up you quit.'

"'Any of you go through that lately?' I ask 'em. None of 'em speaks up.

"'And, if you take Sundays off,' says Campos, 'they accuse you of not wanting to work. And you get fired.'

"'You know anyone that's been fired for that lately?' I want to know. Nobody says anything.

"'Or they bring up your age,' says Comacho. 'They compare you with the young braceros. They tell you you're too old to work. That's happened to me a lot.'

"'Lately?' I ask. He shakes his head.

"'But the most ridiculous argument,' says Ledesma, 'the one that really drives you crazy, is that we don't know how to do the job. I been picking lemons thirty-five years. One day they fire me because I have no skill in lemons. To take my place, they bring in a bracero who never picked a lemon in his life.'

"'Did that happen lately?' I ask him. He shakes his head. I explain the difference, Fred, between ancient beefs and something that's 'pan caliente.' Still hot. And how we gotta be real careful the first time we start raising hell so we don't make jackasses out of ourselves.

"'Well, how about the law?' says this forty-year-old guy, Marin. 'The law says the growers are supposed to hire the "locals" first. But they don't. Lotta times, they'll tell you there's no work. And yet, right there in front of you are the braceros, working away.'

"'So what do you do about it?' I wanna know.

"'Nothing,' says Chavira. 'You start raising hell, you'll never work.' Soon as he says that, Fred, this tight useless feeling at not being able to get a handle on this thing eases off a little bit. Now I can see at least one reason why they aren't making any headway. I can also see how I can help 'em and how that probably ties in with the other, that 'Key' I've been trying to find.

"'Well,' I tell him kind of softly, 'you aren't working anyway, are you?' He gets this kind of half-smile on his face and shrugs. It's a kind of low blow, I know. But I figure I might as well help 'em begin to get ready, Fred, for the fight they're gonna have to make.

"'But, going back to what Marin said,' says Comacho, 'law or no law, those growers and labor contractors are going to give the braceros preference over us. First place, they are single men, and they will room and board 'em and make money on that. Then they will take kickbacks for the jobs they give 'em. So the family man—which is all of us—doesn't stand a chance.'

"By then, it's getting late, Fred, and I can see I'm not going to get any real issues out of 'em. I can't let 'em leave, though, without giving them something to do, or at least to think about, so I try another tack.

"'OK, so they prefer the braceros. But supposing they sent all the braceros back to Mexico. Would there be enough "locals" to do the work?'

"'Oh, sure,' they all chimed in.

"'About how many of 'em are there?' I ask. The thing is bothering the hell out of me. I wanna know!

"'You mean here in Ventura County?' says Campos. I nod. 'Oh, I'd say at least a thousand.'

"'More,' several murmur.

"'What, then—fifteen hundred?'

"'At least that,' says Mejia.

"'Where are they all?' I ask.

"'Quien sabe?' says Campos. 'Who knows? All over the place. I know plenty of 'em.' The others all start nodding. What they're doing, Fred, they're padding the thing a little bit to make me take 'em more seriously. That's when I get this idea:

"'You all have friends who can't get jobs, right?' They all nod. 'All right, why don't we mimeograph some forms and all of you can go out and get the names of everyone you know that needs a job. That way we'll find out how big this "army" we're going to start working with really is.'

"Well, Fred, they aren't too enthusiastic, but they agree. I figure it's a pretty good idea myself. For one thing, it's the only way I know to find out how much they're exaggerating the problem. Second place, it'll keep them all busy doing something until we get that real 'hot issue' and, at the same time, bring them deeper into C.S.O., you know. Third place, it'll sort of hold 'em off a little longer and give me a chance to think about it, so that when we do go into it, we won't be operating completely off the seat of our pants. Which is what I was after in the first place, I guess."

Chapter 6

The Hot Issue

"The Service Center Hut is jammed, as usual, this particular morning. I'm helping this guy get some back wages a grower owes him when the door bangs open and an icy wind blows Mejia and the four other farm workers in and across the room to the five-gallon coffee urn in the corner. They just kind of huddle around it, holding their hands against the hot sides, shivering.

"Old man Garcia lays down his broom and goes over to them: 'Could it be,' he asks, 'that Mr. Zamora was able to resist the magic of the little Referral Card again?' He's got this sort of surprised look of a deadpan comedian on his face.

"'A-a-h,' Chavira kind of shrugs. 'That damned Zamora! You know what he did this morning? 'Pretty slow today,' he says. And we had just seen him send ten truckloads of braceros out to work!'

"'Ay,' says the old man. 'Hearing the same thing every day the way you do, I would die of boredom.'

"'It is a custom we are trying to lose,' says one of the others. 'In Texas where the braceros do not come, you always get up to go to get a job in the morning. So now, here in Oxnard, the habit is still strong within you. The only difference is that—now you always get up to go out to not get a job in the morning.' They all kind of chuckle and go on to other topics.

"That is the way it was, Fred, since the meeting of the Employment Committee. That night they sort of 'discovered' the C.S.O. office. They felt welcome there. Now, they come in every day—not to get help—just to come in with this sort of beat-dog look and sit there while we work on the troubles of all of the other people, but never on theirs.

"'You bring in any more names?' Garcia asks them. He's collecting the names for this little drive I told you we started to see how many unemployed farm workers there are.

"'Para qué?' Chavira asks, 'What for?' Even before he comes out with it, I know that it is coming; and, of course, he is right. What's the sense of bringing in the names of a lot of down-and-out farm workers, so we can get the proof there's a lot of down-and-out farm workers, when we already know there's a lot of down-and-out farm workers? None. We shouldn't have even started it. No issue.

"So, every day I'm sitting there feeling lousier and lousier, wondering what the hell we're going to do, but never moving. Then, on this particular day, it suddenly hits me. What I'd been doing, Fred, I'd been putting it off because these five guys don't come in and say, 'Look, Chavez, I got this employment problem; help me!' You know, make me help 'em the way the others do who come to the office. And I start thinking what a lousy way to treat these guys, and how I gotta do *something*—when the door bangs open again, and here comes this guy, Augustine Lopez.

"'Where's Chavez?' he yells, tearing past Garcia and up to me. He's a lemon worker, and he's hotter than a hornet.

"'What's wrong, Mr. Lopez?' I ask him.

"'Wrong!' he barks. 'They fired me!'

"'How come?' I notice the five guys by the coffee urn are edging over toward us.

"'A-a-h,' he flings his hand in the air. 'They say work's over. No more work 'til lemon season starts again.'

"'They lay everybody off?' I ask him.

"'Hell, no!' he bellows. 'Just us six "locals." There's braceros all over the place. (Remember, Fred, what I told them the other night about the 'hot issue'? Well, here it is.)

"'How long you been in the lemons?' I ask him.

"'Nearly twenty years,' he says, muttering something at the other farm workers. But I'm already on the phone calling the State Farm Placement Service. Some guy named Turner answers. He calls the lemon company and gets back to me.

"'Well, Chavez,' he says, 'Lopez wasn't laid off at all. He quit.' Wow! When he says that, Fred, I start getting hotter than ever. Not only because I know it's a damned lie, but because of the way he says it, like he was right there at the ranch when it happened, and saw the guy quit with his own eyes. Like the company absolutely *has* to be right, for God's sake!

"Well, Fred, I don't say anything. I don't want to insult this guy Turner while there's still a chance he'll help us. So while he's still saying 'Mr. Chavez? Are you still there, Mr. Chavez?' I thank him and slowly hang up the phone and move out from behind the desk.

"'Let's go, Mr. Lopez,' I tell him.

"'Where?' he wants to know.

"'Farm Placement,' I tell him, pushing past the other five farm workers. Then it hits me and I look back at them, motioning: 'Come on, you guys.

We'll all go up together.'

"'N-a-a,' says the young guy, Chavira. 'What's the use?' He really wants to go, you know—they all do. But they've been through it all before and they've about half given up trying. With Lopez, it's all new and he's hot. He still has hope.

"'Come on,' I tell 'em. 'I just want you to go so you can help me find out what gives up there. You know, the Referral Cards and all the rest of it. Are you afraid?'

"'No!' Chavira sort of jerks up his head. 'We're not afraid.'

"'Okay.' I step through the door with all of them right behind me. 'Here we go.'

"Well, Fred, I don't expect to do 'em much good, of course. In a way, it's more like doing 'em a special favor. Kind of making up to them for not being able to really do 'em any good. And, at the same time, making me feel a lot better about it myself."

They had gone to the Employment Office in Ventura, where the Farm Placement Service was located. The F.P. was simply a tiny space with a counter across the middle, five or six folding chairs in front of the counter, and two guys and a desk behind it. The rest of the space was occupied by the Unemployment Compensation people.

"Well, Fred, we walk up to this chubby young guy, Turner, and I brief him a little bit on C.S.O. and the work. I'm starting in on the Lopez case when he stops me:

"'Chavez, I already told you about what the company said about the Lopez case.'

"'Yeah,' I come back at him, 'but six other guys were laid off at the same time as Lopez and they are willing to testify to this.' (I was bluffing, of course.)

"'Look, Chavez,' Turner says, 'this matter is out of my jurisdiction. I just made that phone call for you this morning as a friendly gesture.'

"'Whose jurisdiction is it then?' I ask him.

"'All you can do,' he says, 'is get an attorney and go to court.'

"He had me there, Fred. I knew it was a damned lie, but what can you do? I didn't know enough yet to argue with him, so I moved on to the case of Chavira and the other guys. 'These five workers,' I tell him, 'were here yesterday for a Referral Card to the Ventura County Farm Workers Association. They wouldn't hire 'em.'

"'Why?' Turner gets this fake surprised look.

"'Well,' I explain, 'this guy Zamora just said there was no work for 'em. But that's not true. The Association's got plenty of work—for the braceros.' I repeat in Spanish what I just said, and ask the workers if it's true. They all nod real fast and hard.

"So I turn around to Turner and tell him: 'When these workers have their Referral Cards, he's supposed to hire them, right?'

"Turner looks at the workers and then at me, and lowers his voice: 'Well, Chavez,' he says, 'you can't believe these guys. If they wanted the work, they'd be working.'

"'Yeah, but gee,' I tell him, 'if they didn't want to work why would they buy some guy's gas to bring them all the way down here from Oxnard to get a Referral Card yesterday? I mean, it doesn't make sense. If they didn't want to work, why would they bother about the Referral Card even?'

"'Well, look,' he motions me over closer to him. 'Some of these guys are bums. They don't want to work, but they pretend they do so people won't know they're just lazy bums.'

"'But these guys have families,' I tell him. 'They aren't bums.'

"'Well, you don't know,' he says, giving me this real shrewd look. 'People can have families and still be bums.' And he lets out this kind of a quick, short whine like a horse.

"I don't like it, Fred, but I don't want to rile the guy. At least not while there's any chance of getting a few, small favors out of him. So I just sort of back away from our little confidential discussion and ask him for some more Referral Cards for all of 'em, including Lopez.

"'Okay,' he kind of shrugs. 'But it's just a waste of government property. They're not going to use them.'

"'Quieren otras tarjetas?' I ask the workers. 'You want some more cards?'

"They all shrug too, just like Turner—but for a different reason, of course. Chavira comes out with his usual: 'Para qué?' I go into this little huddle with 'em and ask 'em to take another card, just so I can see what happens.

"'Está bien. No me importa,' says Chavira. Like, 'We're here. Nothing to lose, I guess.'

"Then Turner pulls out these big Employment Application forms. They're the kind they use in factories, where you have to put down the whole damned story of your life: where you worked the last ten years, kind of work, wages. Name it. I can just see us practically all day long in that damned office, so I ask him:

"'You mean we have to fill out all this just to get a Referral Card?' He nods. 'But golly,' I go, kinda sad, 'that'll take hours and these guys have wasted half a day already. They wanna go to work right now.'

"'That's the procedure,' he shrugs. 'Take it or leave it.'

"What I wanna do, Fred, I wanna wad it up and throw it in his face. But I don't. I just join the 'shrugging party' and make out the damned forms for the guys. In about two hours, Turner hands us the cards. On each one, he's written the name of a different association: Somis Labor Association, Tafoya Company, etc. They're all the way to hell and gone, out in the boonies.

"'Hey,' I kinda groan, 'these guys can't go way out there. They have no transportation. How about the Association in Oxnard?'

"Turner says, 'Oh, uh—well,' and sort of swings his head around toward his boss, Bates, and back. 'We don't have any orders from them right at the present,' he tells me.

"'But I thought that anyone that has braceros has to take "locals," I tell him. And still looking right at him, I throw him this thing I had read: 'Isn't that what Public Law 78 says?'

"The second I say that, Turner starts turning red and takes another quick look over his shoulder again at Bates. Then he grabs the cards and mumbles, 'Well, all right then, I'll change 'em.'

"'They always pull that,' says Chavira, walking beside me towards the car. 'They're afraid of Zamora, I think, and they know he don't want us. Also, they know we've only got one car between us so they try to send each of us to a separate job knowing we have no way of getting to work, so we won't even be able to go out to get turned down for a job.'

"Forty-five minutes later, we pull up at the Association in Oxnard. Some old bald-headed guy stops us right at the gate.

"'That's old Pelon,' says Chavira. 'Zamora's dispatcher.'

"'What do you guys want?' Pelon yells.

"'Jobs,' I yell back, killing the engine.

"He shakes his head. 'Time's past for that. You want to work? Be here at five o'clock in the morning.'

"'How about just leaving our Referral Cards?' I ask him.

"'What for?' Pelon smiles. 'They're no good. They're outdated. You want to work tomorrow, you gotta get a card with tomorrow's date on it.'

"'I can't hardly believe it,' I told him. 'You mean we gotta go all the way back to the Farm Placement again?' He just nods and walks back to the Association office.

"'Hell!' I start the car and take off for Ventura again. 'Turner must have known that'd happen.'

"'How not?' Chavira says. 'Even I knew.' I shoot him a look through the rear-view mirror and he shows his real white teeth. 'Well,' he says, 'you wanted to learn.' They all start laughing, and Chavira says with seriousness: 'Sure, that's part of the little game they play with us. They figure if they keep us going back and forth enough, maybe we'll get discouraged.' He swings around towards the guys in the back seat and asks 'em: 'Am I right?'

"In the rear-view mirror I can see the four of them back there nodding. Watching them, all at once I get this hot tingling, thinking how maybe I've found some guys like the ones who work with the little-guy-with-the-bottle. The ones who 'all believe the same way.'

"Even before we get up to the counter, Turner calls out to us: 'Well, Chavez, back already?'

"'Yeah.' I kind of bark out what happened.

"'Oh, that's a shame.' He gives this little clicking sound with his teeth and shakes his head. 'Well, it's probably just a little misunderstanding.' He pulls out some more of those Employment Application forms. 'Have 'em fill these out and we'll fix 'em up so they can go to work in the morning.'

"'What do you mean?' I ask him. 'We already filled those out this morning.'

"'No, he says, 'those were for today.' And he goes into all this gobbledegook, as you call it, Fred, about how every time a guy applies for work, he's got to make out a new form, because the guy may have worked since he made out the old form, and they have to have a record of that in order to keep the case 'current' all the time, so that gobble, gabble, gibble, gooble!

"Well, that starts another little argument. I ask him how come he doesn't add the new stuff to the old form and save all that time, and he tells me about 'government procedure' again. And again I start to blow, and tamp it down. In the end, we spend another two hours making out those damned forms, and get the Referral Cards, and take off.

"Fred, they had me doing this every morning for forty days, even though, as we found out later, the law doesn't require it at all. With some of the guys, I had been through it so many times I didn't have to ask them for their history anymore: I knew it by heart.

"We're just leaving Ventura when I turn to Chavira: 'You know what?' I tell him. "We haven't got anything better to do, how about hitting up some of those other associations for a job and see what they tell us?' I'm hot as hell on this thing by now, Fred, and I want to see if it's really as bad as they say it is.

"'Oh, you can't do that,' says Chavira. 'You've got to get a Referral

Card to each one.'

"'To hell with that noise!' I tell him, turning off Highway 101 into the farming area. 'What we'll do, when we come up to them, we'll just flash these cards at them, ask them for a job, and see what they say. Any of 'em have any seriousness about hiring you, we can always go back to the F.P. (by now that's what we're all calling Farm Placement) and get another Referral Card. If the job pays enough to make it worthwhile to buy the gas to get there.

But of course, they never had to come to grips with that "if." They hit the larger associations, such as Somis (which Cesar had toured me through one time) and Buena Vista and Oxnard Plains—and it was, "Sorry, no help needed." Or, "Maybe later on." Or, "We'll notify Farm Placement when we're ready."

Going on to the smaller companies—the Lemoneira and two other lemon outfits, two of the Japanese associations, and Hovely Company— the welcome they got was exactly the same: a solid "No go" wall. Meantime, of course, the braceros had been so thick around the place they were practically crawling out from under the rocks.

Thinking that *somewhere* there had to be some little dinky outfit that wasn't playing the game, Cesar kept on. They had driven way out in the boonies and found the same identical thing. Either the straight turndown, or some stupid little dodge to get rid of them. And always the stinging barb at the end about "how closely I'm working with F.P."

"Well, by the time we got back to the Hut, around six p.m., I'm feeling pretty bad. Chavira and the other five guys are very nice about it, but it keeps eating on me anyway. I feel like I took up their time, and well—we didn't do anything. I feel like I have to apologize, tell 'em how sorry I am, how I wish I could have gotten them some jobs, and how it woulda probably been better if we had not gone out there and wasted their time, you know.

"All of 'em just sort of shift around in their chairs, except Chavira. 'That's all right, Chavez,' he grins. 'We understand. It's not the first time, you know. We've gone through it all before. Many times. So don't worry about us.'

"'You mean,' I ask him, 'that we've still got that appointment with your pal Zamora in the morning?' They all give me a big grin, and go off down the street, kidding each other.'"

Chapter 7

The Rat Race

Next morning, when Cesar had pulled up to the Hut, it looked like a little igloo hiding there in the four o'clock fog. But no Eskimos. Figuring that the guys had decided to forget about it, he started for the door and all but bumped into five bright orange dots. There they were—the five old faithfuls—back beneath the overhang, smoking. Lopez never showed up, but a half-hour later, after taking on some coffee, Cesar and the others drove through the Association gate.

Just as they pulled into the yard, things started to click—like clock-work. On one side were fifty numbered trucks of the type they used for troop transport. On the other, hundreds of braceros. In the middle, inside the office, stood Pelon, yelling the names and numbers of the bracero crews into the PA squawk-box.

"'Cuadrilla número una, los Liones!' he yells. 'Crew number one, the Lions! Cuadrilla número dos, los Tigeres! Numero tres, los Galgos! Véngase!' He motions to them. 'Come on! Vámonos!' He cups his hands. 'Let's go!'

"Chavira lets out this short laugh: 'Lions and tigers and greyhounds!' he grunts. 'Imagine how those poor devils must have bust their ass to earn nicknames like that!'

"About then, the trucks roar off, the mess-hall door bangs open, and this whole mob of braceros comes pouring up to the Association office. 'Hey, Chavez,' Chavira nudges me, 'see that other guy in the office?' He points to a light-complexioned little pouter pigeon with a handlebar mustache, behind the counter in front of a long line of braceros. 'That's the big honcho, Zamora.'

The place was so jammed that Cesar and the "locals" hadn't been able to reach the office, so they had just stood there taking in the scene. Whenever Pelon had stopped for breath, they could catch Zamora's voice in the background, talking to some bracero who was begging him for a job.

"God! you shoulda heard this Zamora, Fred: 'No, Gonzales!' he kinda snarls. 'You're not due today; you worked yesterday!' As Gonzales moves along, head down, another guy steps up to the Big Man: 'What are you talking about, Grijalva? Lemme see, you worked yesterday. You're not due 'til day after tomorrow.'

"'How come they have so many more than they need?' I ask Chavira.

"'That's easy,' Chavira tells me, 'any of 'em don't kiss the Big Man's ass, or bust his own, he loses out to somebody else.' Then he points to a bunch of candy, pop and cigarette machines along the wall. 'Guess who gets a kickback on them? On the food, too.' He cocks his head toward the office: 'The Big Man in there. So you see, the more braceros he herds, the more money in his own pocket.'

"'How'd you find out all this?' I ask him.

"He points toward the mess hall: 'See that guy with the white cap back at the stove? He's a buddy of mine. Also a friend of Zamora's—as long as he keeps getting his kickback.'

"By seven a.m., the last bracero is gone, and we move up in front of Zamora. He's had his eye on us for a long time. Now, leaning there on his elbows on the counter, he takes the cards from the five farm workers and throws them into a box.

"'Too late,' he says, starting to walk away. 'Should have been here at five o'clock.'

"'Wait a minute!' I push past the farm workers. 'We were here at 4:30, and you know it. I saw you giving us the eye. You just made sure you got to those other guys first.'

"'Who are you?' He gives me this beady-eyed look. After I tell him, he studies me a minute, and then slams his hand down on the counter: 'Not my fault you let them crowd you out. You want to work, come back tomorrow.' And he swings away through the door behind the counter.

"Back at the Hut, I'm so pissed I can hardly dial the damn numbers getting through to Turner.

"'Hold it a minute, Chavez,' he says when he hears what happened. 'I'll see what the Association says. There's always two sides to a coin, you know.' He hangs up, and five minutes later he's on the line again: 'Well, Chavez,' he gets this kind of patient tone in his voice, 'Mr. Zamora claims you didn't even go out there this morning.'

"This is just so awful, it catches me clear off-guard: 'Buh . . . buh . . .' I kind of sputter, yelling, "But the workers gave him their cards.'

"'Maybe so, Chavez,' he says, 'but Mr. Zamora told me there were no "locals" there at all this morning. Exactly none.'

"'He's lying!' I yell. 'I was right there and saw the whole thing myself.'

"'Well, I don't know, Chavez,' he comes back. 'Mr. Hayes has known Mr. Zamora ever since he was head Compliance Officer for the government's bracero program around here, and—'

"As he goes on giving me this shit about what a prince of a guy this little prick is, I gradually begin to get a dim idea how rotten the whole thing is. What it is, Fred, it's a system—a real nice, sweet, closed system. With full cooperation on both sides."

"So it's not only the growers you've had to fight," I said, "but the State guys too?"

"That's right, Fred, and I'm also beginning to get a little scared. But there's just enough cloak-and-dagger stuff on the grower side to make you feel that, sooner or later, they'll slip up and we'll be able to get something on them and make it stick. 'Course, what you're trying to do, you're trying to build up your hopes.

"So pretty quick, Fred, I just accidentally on purpose disconnect on Turner. Right away Chavira wants to know what we're going to do next. It's one of those times when you kinda 'go deaf' because you haven't got an answer, and you want to sort of give yourself a little extra time to dream one up.

"'Huh?' I kinda groan. While he's repeating his question, the door opens and in comes Soria with some more farm workers—Mejia, old man Campos, and a few others. I get 'em all around me and give the ones that just came in a quickie fill-in on what happened at the Association. As I'm finishing, up pops that little answer I've been looking for:

"'Now what we could do,' I tell them, 'we could get a gang of the guys in cars and make a kind of parade up to the Farm Placement and all over the county. You know, sort of a "Caravan of Unemployed Farm Workers."'

"'What for?' asks old Campos.

"'Well, uh—you know,' I make this kind of a vague motion with my hand. 'To put more pressure on the Farm Placement for one thing. Also to let the rest of the workers know we're "vivito y coliando," you know. Alive and kicking. What do you say?' I lean forward looking at each one of them real fast. I'm pretty damned excited, but hell! I don't know why we ought to do it, really. It's just that I know we've started this thing, we gotta keep the workers going, you know, moving, doing *something*.

"For about five seconds nobody says anything—like it's some new thing they're trying to fit into what they know. Then Chavira lets out this little chuckle: 'Whatta we got to lose?' he shrugs. 'Let's go!' That must be what they are all waiting for because, as soon as he comes out with it, the rest get fired up, jump in the cars, and off we go again to the street corners, the railroad tracks, the pool halls, and the barber shops, corraling workers."

At first, they had been reluctant to go. Then, infused with the same excitement that had juiced up their captors, the victims had finally lept into the cars and, a half-hour later, were part of a block-long parade down a Ventura sidewalk and into the Farm Placement office—Cesar with his old World War II Navy pea jacket in the lead.

"It's quite a sight, Fred, but Bates and Turner just look sort of bored. Like what the hell can a little handful a' 'locals' do against the System? But we get a little revenge on 'em anyway, making 'em miss their lunch hour waiting for us to fill out the Employment Applications. When they ask which ranch we want the Referral Card for, I just sort of answer automatically, 'Oxnard Association.' I don't know why, exactly. Who cares whether they don't get this nice dream-job on one big nowhere ranch or some other one? Nobody. No difference."

Then, with Cesar in the lead, their motorcade toured Ventura County, past miles of broccoli, hundreds of acres of flowers and celery and tomato seedlings. There were crews of two and three hundred braceros in every field. Where the braceros were far off, the "locals" had joked about the way they were "busting ass." Where they were close to the road, the "locals" fell very quiet, their eyes following the long line of braceros hungrily.

"In about an hour, Fred, we get to the Oxnard Association. It's real quiet. Nobody's around at all now but old Pelon standing by the gate. I don't even slow down—just gun it on through past Pelon and clear up to the office, with all the other cars slamming in behind.

"Old Pelon tries to bar the way, but we just push past him through the door and right up to where Zamora is standing by the counter.

"'OK,' I tell him, 'we have the cards. We wanna work.'

"Zamora got this real bored look on his puss. 'Look, you guys, I haven't got time for you. You want to work, you gotta be here at five o'clock in the morning.'

"'Now wait,' I tell him. 'We were here at five o'clock this morning and you told Turner we weren't here at all.'

"'You calling me a liar?' he says.

"'No, I'm not calling you a liar. But you know it's not true, because we were here and we talked to you.'

"'Look,' he says, 'I can hire whoever I want to. I don't have to hire you people.'

"'Well, but according to Public Law 78—'

"'Aw, don't give me that shit!' he cuts in. 'I'm busy, and I'm running this Association. If you want a job, you have to follow my rules.

Otherwise, we won't bother with you.'

"'By now I'm pretty upset, but I'm trying to keep my temper down. 'Look, sir,' I tell him, 'I don't know why you won't hire these "locals." But I know one thing—they should be hired before the braceros. And another thing I know—you have an awful lot of braceros and the people with me here really need the work.' Then I go into the business of how they have families and kids and they're hungry, you know. But hell! I'm wasting my time.

"'If they're so hungry,' he sorta sneers, 'they better get out here on time so they can get some work and earn some money.'

"'Will you promise you'll hire 'em if we're here in the morning?' I ask him.

"'I'm not promising nothing,' he says, 'you just come in the morning. Take your chances with the rest of 'em and now, get out of here! I'm busy.'

"'No,' I tell him. 'We're not leaving until you tell us. So just tell us so we can leave.'

"He looks up real quick. 'Why? Where are you going?'

"'We know where to go.' I give him my best sly look. (This is a big bluff, Fred. We haven't got the dimmest idea.)

"'OK, I've had enough. You guys get out of this office!' He points his finger toward the door.

"I shake my head. 'Not until you tell us you'll hire us, or you won't. One or the other.'

"'Nope,' he shakes his head, 'come back tomorrow morning.'

"I stare straight at him. 'You hire us right now, or promise you'll hire us in the morning.'

"'Look,' he sorta springs away from the wall where he's been leaning and bends down toward me, over the counter. 'You trying to be a wise guy or something?'

"All this time, John's been standing behind me with the workers, watching Zamora. Now, all at once, there's this low growl and I just have time to step aside as John comes charging by like he's 'hitting the line' and knocks the counter over trying to grab Zamora. 'You son of a bitch!' he yells.

"Zamora jumps back just in time and tears through the door behind the counter. Then he sticks his head back out and yells at his secretary: 'Ca—ca—call someone!'

"'Who, Mr. Zamora?' she screams.

"'I don't care. Anyone!' Then he slams the door, and you can hear the key turning as he locks himself in.

"As we are walking out, I turn to El Giganton (that's what the workers all call John, the 'super-giant'). 'No, John,' I tell him. 'Don't ever do that again.' He starts to give me an argument so I pull him to one side: 'Look, John, these guys can send us to jail.'

"'What's wrong with that?' he wants to know. 'That's how you build up a following.'

"'Sure,' I tell him. 'The people will follow us right up to the front steps of the jail. But that's as far as they'll go. And if we get canned, that's the end of it. Especially now at the very beginning of this thing.'

"'Awh, you're afraid!' he says.

"'No, John, I'm not afraid to be in jail. 'Specially for a cause like this. In fact, I think it would be good later on. But right now, if they throw both of us in jail, the people won't follow us. Then we lose everything. It's finished.'

"As I'm getting into the car, Zamora comes up. 'Who's Chavez?' he wants to know. (I guess he called Farm Placement and they probably reminded him who I am.)

"'I'm Chavez,' I tell him.

"'Come over here,' he says very softly.

"'What do you want? You going to give us a job?'

"'Come inside,' he says, motioning toward the office.

"'Ay, para adentro, todos,' I tell the workers. 'All of us inside.'

"'Oh, no,' Zamora shakes his hand at me. 'Just you.'

"'Oh, no,' I tell him. 'You won't trick me! From now on, everything between us will be in front of the workers.'

"'Well,' he says, 'I just wanted to let you know that, well—both of us lost our tempers.'

"'No, Mr. Zamora. I did not lose my temper.'

"'Well, both of us . . . .'

"'No,' I cut in. 'Let's get this straight. I did *not* lose my temper. You insulted me.'

"'Well, you know how it is.' He holds out his hands, palms up.

"'Look, I did not lose my temper, and I didn't say anything. You insulted me and I think you owe me an apology for that.'

"'Well, you know how those things are,' he says, shrugging. 'But maybe one of these days, we'll get together for a cup a coffee.'

"'Maybe so,' I tell him. 'Someday when you have a lot of coffee, we'll get together with these workers and have some. Meantime, I think you should give 'em all a job.'

"'Naw,' he says. 'Like I told you before, I don't have to give anybody a job unless I want to.'

"I start the car and lean out the window. 'Well, someday we're going to make you give 'em a job.' Zamora goes back inside shaking his head, and John comes over to the car.

"'So what are we going to do now?' He stands there with his big hands on his hips, looking at the ground.

"I look back to where the workers are standing around the cars. 'Well, I guess there's only one thing to do: just go back to the Farm Placement and protest.'

"'But hell, Cesar!' His voice heated up. 'You tried that and what good'd it do?' Then he takes this deep breath and hunches his head down in his shoulders like he's getting ready for an off-tackle play: 'We gotta blast this whole damn system wide open!'

"'What do you mean, John?' I ask him. 'Like a strike, or something?'

"'Oh, no,' he shakes this big head of his back and forth. 'That's been tried. It didn't work. What I mean is something really big.'

"'Well, like what?' I ask him.

"He swings that head from side to side, sort of like a lion looking for the guy that just wounded him. 'Hell, I don't know, Cesar! That's what we've got to figure out.' All at once I get this feeling that what John wants is some kind of miracle. Not just a smooth one, though. A miracle and, on top of that, a super-atomic explosion!

"'Maybe you're right, John.' I put my hand on his shoulder. 'But between now and the time we get it figured, there's only two things I know to do: we gotta keep the workers moving now that we got 'em going on this thing; and we gotta keep the pressure on the Farm Placement and the Association.'

Of course, Cesar had known he wasn't going to get too far merely protesting to those people. It had simply been that or nothing. He had to keep hammering, pestering away with the absolute resolution that he would do it, until someday something would just have to give. In a way, it had been much like the battles he'd had years before with the Registrars of Voters in Kern and Santa Clara counties, finally forcing them to permit C.S.O. leaders to register Chicanos to vote.

But when he had told the workers about returning to Farm Placement, there was a sudden loss of interest. They began to mumble about how they had to catch up with some contractor who had promised them a day's work in the celery. Or they had to arrange a ride to work the following day, in the carrots—to make a buck six bits! Or something.

In any case, by the time Cesar had left for Ventura, it had boiled down to Mejia, Campos, Chavira, and John—and just enough others to fill his station wagon. That's when he got his first little hint about how hard it was going to be to keep the workers going around that damned Rat Race day after day.

Chapter 8

Upstairs

"Back at the F.P., Turner tells me, 'Well, I don't know what I can do about all this.' He's standing there looking down at the counter. Then he gives me kind of a half-smile: 'I'm just the low man on the totem pole around here.'

"'Oh,' I tell him, 'well, then maybe we'd better go a little higher up the pole, uh?'

"He rolls his eyes back towards Bates sitting at the desk behind him. I guess Bates must have heard us, because now he comes up beside Turner.

"'All right,' he yaps, 'I heard the whole thing. Now what do you want?' Bates is kinda tall and skinny with a face like a skeleton, and these real thick-lensed glasses that make you think you're looking through two holes—right into his brain.

"'What do we want?' I look at him like that's a pretty stupid question. 'We want you to make the Association hire these guys.'

"'Nah!' He sorta waves me away. 'I'm not meddling in the Association's business. How do I know you guys are giving me a straight story?'

"John's still spoiling for a fight, Fred. Before I can stop him, he leans over me and shoves his big head down towards Bates: 'Listen, you,' his eyelids sorta slit together. 'Are you calling us liars or something?'

"Bates' head kinda straightens back real quick: 'I'm not calling anybody anything,' he says. 'But as far as I'm concerned, it's just your word against Mr. Zamora's, and . . . .'

"'Sure,' John sneers, 'the word of the Association against the workers. That's the "word" you're talking about! Now, look, Bates,' his big finger comes down like a club in front of Bates' nose, 'we've been taking this shit from you and Hayes and your whole stinking outfit long enough. Now you either start living up to the law, or there's gonna be big trouble!'

For a moment, no one had said anything. The workers stood there watching John as though they were in a trance. Cesar nudged John, trying to calm him down. Bates, glaring at John, appeared to be right on the rim of blowing his top. Just then, a smartly dressed Chicano came smiling in, giving Bates the sign he wanted to see him.

"'Listen, Mr. Whatever-your-name-is.' Bates sort of pulls himself together. 'You are going to learn that threats will get you exactly nowhere in this office.' Then he turns to Turner: 'They're all yours. If you want to waste your time with them, OK. I've got more important things to do.' And he takes off towards this snappily dressed Chicano.

"John makes a move like he's gonna go after him, but I grab his arm and turn to Turner: 'Kinda left you holding the bag, didn't he?' I kid him.

"'Yeah,' he says, 'or the "buck." See what I mean by my being the low man on the totem pole around here?'

"'Well,' I kind of grin, 'the farm worker's the low man, too, you know. Maybe we'd better get together. "Hombre, sin hombre, no vale nada," I tell him in Spanish. 'We either hang together or separately.'

"That little bit of Spanish really gets to him, Fred, and he tells me how he always wanted to learn the 'lingo.' I laugh and tell him sure, that sort of proves what I just said about how we can help each other. Of course, while I'm buttering him up, I can hear old John talking with the workers. They aren't listening much, though. It's like they want to see who wins, me or him.

"Anyway, pretty quick Turner picks up the phone: 'It's probably going to be useless,' he says, 'but let's see what Mr. Zamora has to say this time.' He cocks his head back, 'Hello, Mr. Zamora, how's everything? Well, we have Mr. Chavez here from this C.S.O. outfit, you know . . . yeah . . . uh-huh . . . Well, he says they took some workers to the Association this afternoon and they weren't hired. Of course, don't get me wrong, Mr. Zamora, I'm not saying you should have hired them if they're not qualified . . . Oh . . . oh . . . I see. Well, in that case . . . fine. All right, Mr. Zamora. OK. I'll see you. Goodbye, Mr. Zamora.'

"He hangs up and shows me the palms of his hands. 'You see, Mr. Chavez, he says the jobs are there, but your people just don't want to work.'

"'Look, Turner,' I can feel my lip trembling a bit. 'Do you think if these guys didn't want to work, they'd keep coming here every day—sometimes two and three times a day, like we've been doing?' He sorta drops his eyes. 'No, Turner,' I say the words real slow. 'That guy's lying and you know it.' I keep looking at him. 'So what are you going to do?'

"He makes this little helpless movement with his hands. 'There's not too much we can do, Chavez. We're mainly a referral agency, you know.'

"'Yeah,' I tell him, 'but according to Public Law 78, it's part of your job to protect the rights of the "locals," isn't it?'

"'That's right—but don't forget, Chavez,' he lowers his voice like he's trying to tell me something without telling me. 'We don't set policy, you know; that comes from upstairs.' He sends this half-scared look over to where Bates is walking out with this well-dressed Chicano.

"Right then, Fred, it's like all at once Turner gets an idea. 'Hey, Chavez,' he whispers, 'you see that guy over there with Mr. Bates? That's Mr. Morales. He's a Compliance Officer with the U.S. Department of Labor. He's the one that can really clamp down on this sort of thing.'

"Of course, Turner is passing the buck on this, Fred. And he's a little scared, too. But he also wants to help, just a little bit, I think, or he wouldn't have bothered with us at all.

"Anyway, this really gets me by surprise. I take another look at Morales and ask Turner, 'Does he work around here?'

"'Sure,' he says. 'He's got an office in Santa Barbara . . . .'

"While he's giving me all this gobbledegook about Morales' duties and I'm trying to pin him down on who's supposed to do what, all at once I get this thought about having all of them, the Farm Placement guys and Morales, come before the whole C.S.O. membership and explain their program to the people, Fred."

I interrupt Cesar—"And so the people can explain their problems to the brass."

"Right," Cesar grins. "And scare the pee out of 'em with their numbers.

"So anyway, Fred, I give the workers my idea, and they go for it. Then, I tell it to Turner.

"Well, he bends his head with this little twist. 'I don't know. You'll have to ask Mr. Bates.' Then he gives me this little wrinkly-eyed look: 'How many of these guys,' he jerks his head towards the workers, 'usually come to your meetings?'

"'Oh, I don't know exactly, five or six hundred anyway.' I'm lying like a bastard, of course. We only had about two hundred and fifty at the last one.

"He just stands there with this little smile. 'Come on, Chavez, you trying to tell me there's five or six hundred unemployed farm workers around here?'

"Well, our membership isn't all farm workers, by a long shot, but being he misunderstood me, I go along with the gag.

"'Oh, hell no!' I tell him. 'Those are just the ones that come to the meeting. You want to take the whole county and all, I figure there's between a thousand and fifteen hundred of them.' ('Course what I'm doing, Fred, I'm trying to win Turner and Bates over to our side a little more and maybe scare them into action.)

"'Naa!' Turner sort of waves me off. 'You'll be lucky if you find fifty unemployed farm workers in the whole area.' I start to object, but he cuts in on me: 'Look, Chavez, if there were fifteen hundred unemployed farm workers around here, it'd cause the biggest stink that ever hit this county. Why, hell! they'd probably declare it a disaster area!' But the way his eyes keep jumping around, I can tell he's a little bit shook up.

"Telling the guys, in Spanish, what's going on, all at once I get pinged by this other little idea: 'Remember that plan we had to record the names of all of the out-of-work farm workers?' They all nod. 'Well, maybe it wouldn't be such a bad idea now to go out and really do it.'

"I can tell by their eyes that *this time* the idea clicks. 'Surely,' says old Campos. 'And while we're registering them, we can push 'em to come to the meeting we're gonna have with these government guys. Imagine! A whole roomful of outawork farm workers! Scare the shit right out of these phonies.'

"'That's a damned good idea!' I tell him, noticing how the others are really excited, all except John, of course.

"Just then, Bates and Morales walk into the office, and Morales starts shooting the breeze with Turner. Bates goes over to his desk, so I go over and hit him up for the meeting. Without even looking up, he just says: 'No, I never accept speaking engagements of that type.'

"'Why not?' I ask.

"'Personal reasons,' he grunts. I'm still pushing him on it, when I notice Morales is leaving. I tell Bates we'll see about those 'personal reasons' later, motion to the guys, and hurry after Morales. He's just going out the door of the front office, when we catch him:

"'Ah, qué tal, muchachos?' he says. 'What's up, boys?'

"'We'd like to talk to you a minute,' I tell him. He's a real handsome guy, almost pretty. He's dark, medium height, with these real dreamy eyes and super-long lashes.

"'Why, certainly,' he nods. 'What is it? Something about the food at the camp mess-hall? Or do you boys want to go back to Mexico?'

"'You've got us wrong,' I tell him, 'we're not braceros. We want to talk business!'

"'Oh. Oh. Well, surely,' he kinda stutters, those long lashes of his starting to blink like crazy, and his eyes looking around the office. 'Come on over here, fellows.' He moves toward some folding chairs in the corner. 'Have a seat.'

"I'm just starting to tell him the problem, when he stops me: 'You fellows from the C.S.O.?' Some of us nod. 'Uh-*huh*.' He clamps down on his upper lip with the lower one and gives us this slow nod. Then he opens his fancy briefcase by his side. 'You see all that?' He flips through a big pile of papers. 'I'm trying to close down one of the Associations right now. Too damned many violations. I'm recommending decertification.' He winks and makes this slow, throat-slitting gesture. 'Cut off their braceros, you know.'

"'Won't they hire the locals?' I wanna know.

"'Oh, no, not *that*!' he almost whispers. 'So far, I've never had to work on *that* kind of a case, thank God! Those growers can really get vicious on stuff like that.' He leans over closer to us: 'They're trying to get me!' he whispers, looking back over both shoulders.

"'Who?' I ask.

"'The Assocation,' he whispers.

"Then he jerks his head toward the door. 'Let's go to La Tupinamba down the street. There's more privacy there!'

"A few minutes later, he folds his hands under his chin on the cantina table. 'Now then,' he says, very relaxed and contented. 'What were we— oh, yes, the Association. Well, brother, the growers aren't going to feed the braceros any of that dehydrated shit while I'm around.'

"'I don't know,' I tell 'im, 'in a way, it's better to eat that than starve like a lot of the "locals" are doing.' I pull out some of the scattered notes I been keeping on our daily 'Rat Race' and read them aloud to him. I'm only about half through the first page, when his eyes start blinking again real fast, and he jumps up and leads us back to a little, empty banquet room clear at the rear.

"'Never know who's listening,' he sorta mutters. After I've read him the rest, he sits there wagging his head back and forth, holding his jaws: 'Broth-*er*!' he finally groans. 'That stuff's dynamite! One job-preference violation after another!' Then he points his finger at me: 'But let me tell you one thing: If you're gonna take on this guy Zamora, be ready. For your own protection, and C.S.O.'s, get all the facts.

"He leans over and looks up and down the corridor. 'Before Zamora got this cushy job with the Association, he used to be State Supervisor of Farm Worker Employment for the Federal Government. So believe me, he knows exactly how far he can go on this job-preference thing without getting into trouble.'

"'That's exactly what we want to talk to you about, Mr. Morales.' I look him straight in the eye.

"'Oh . . . oh, well—' His eyes start batting faster'n ever now. 'See, fellows, I can't get involved in this sort of thing. Not in the initial stages, anyway.'

"'What do you mean?' I ask him. 'Turner told us you're the big "IT" in all this stuff.'

"'No, no, no.' He shakes his head real fast. 'Farm Placement has jurisdiction here. They try to adjust the case. If they bog down somewhere along the line, then we come in.'

"For a minute, I just sit there looking down at the table, shaking my head. Then I go after him: 'You guys are just kicking us back and forth between you. They tell us one thing; you tell us the opposite. What's going on around here, anyway!'

"Morales just sorta shrugs, fluttering those long eyelashes. 'OK!' I finally tell him. 'There's only one way to straighten this thing out: you'll just have to come to our next membership meeting and explain to the workers what this is all about.'

"'You'll have to clear that with Farm Placement,' he says. 'I can't barge in on any local meetings unless they invite me.'

"'Still passing the buck, uh?' I tell him, sliding out of the booth. 'Well, that buck stops someplace, Morales. And I'm going to find out where!' We pile outa there and head back to Oxnard."

"So then, Cesar, it wasn't just the growers and the State of California you were bucking," I said. "You had to go up against the Feds too, uh?"

"That's right," said Cesar. "I could hardly wait to get back to Oxnard and phone the big honchos in Sacramento to force these local guys to come to our meeting. For one thing, I wanna show up that tight-assed Bates and throw a nice big monkeywrench into that cute little game Turner and Morales are playing. But the main thing, Fred, we've got this issue now; and getting 'em up there before the members'll give us a chance to put on a terrific demonstration against them and the whole lousy system!"

At the Hut that afternoon, the Employment Committee had elected James Flores as permanent Chairman and held a quickie meeting to approve the plan for the Unemployed Farm Workers' Registration Drive and the mass meeting confrontation with the State and Federal brass. Then they put in a call to Edward Hayes, State Director of the Farm Placement Service, to try and get him to "direct" Bates and Turner to come to that meeting. The Committee was just adjourning when Hayes' return call came through. Cesar took it: "'Hold the line, please, Mr. Chavez.' It's Hayes' secretary. Hell! I'm not exactly building any hopes on this call, Fred. What we decided was to call Hayes first, probably get the brushoff, and then use it against him.

"'Hayes speaking,' comes this rough, sorta bored voice through the phone. I'm just starting to tell him what we want when he breaks in on me:

'No, Chavez, that sorta thing is completely out. We don't pay our people to go around making speeches. I'm sorry.'

"'OK.' I'm just as cool as cool. 'If that's the way you want it, Mr. Hayes . . .' I click him off and get ahold of some guy in the Governor's office. Well, Fred, he's just going into this 'the-Governor's-very-busy' routine, when I wink at the workers gathered around my desk and cut in on him: 'Well, you just tell Governor Pat Brown for us how much the Spanish-speaking people appreciate all the help he and the rest of the Democrats are giving us!' And I bang him off.

"Then I shoot off a straight wire to the Governor and get Tony Rios to send one, as National C.S.O. President, in the name of the whole C.S.O. movement. With a little reminder at the end about the three hundred and fifty thousand Mexican Americans we've registered to vote in California!"

Governor Brown had immediately referred the matter back to F.P. Director Hayes, which was pretty much the equivalent of what the L.A. Police Chief had done in 1952 when he sent the cop who beat Tony Rios to investigate the beating! Cesar's answering wire had read: "Hayes unacceptable." An hour later, the Governor had replied: "Matter referred to John Carr, Director, State Employment Service, Hayes' immediate superior." In high spirits, Cesar had arranged for Chairman Tony Del Buono to call an immediate meeting of the Oxnard C.S.O. Executive Committee to take action on the Employment Committee's plan for the Registration of Unemployed Farm Workers and for the mass membership meeting to climax it.

"You know how it is in an organization, Fred. All you have to do is bring up something loaded with a little dynamite and all the armchair philosophers and 'developed leaders' try to defuse it. No sooner does James Flores present the plan than the hassle begins.

"'But what's the point, Cesar?' Del Buono wantsa know. 'We'll just be stirring up a lotta trouble and making the workers think we're gonna get 'em jobs, when you know we're not gonna do any such thing. Not by registering them, anyway, or trying to involve 'em in that "Rat Race" of yours. So what we're doing, we're lying to them, Cesar. Besides,' he chuckles, 'you're not going to get them to go with you on your daily journey anyway. They've been that route.'

"'Maybe so,' I tell him. 'But have you got a better plan?' He just shrugs, and I look around at the others. 'We're committed to helping the farm workers, aren't we?' Most of 'em nod. 'All right, how we gonna do it? The final answer's not around, but at least with this plan that James presented it'll give us a chance to keep moving and stirring up the workers.

"'Then if we keep at it long enough, maybe we'll be able to help some of the workers in the row-crops get the same thing that the locals have got in the lemons. If we can once get something like that, then, when we finally get job preference for locals on every ranch in this county, we'll have the guys all organized to move right in and go to work.'

"Next it's the union turn, Fred: 'No, Cesar,' says Rachel Guajardo. 'Tony Del Buono's right. You won't get the workers to go with you on this. You know why? Because these jobs in the fields don't pay enough. They don't want 'em. What we've got to fight for is a living wage!'

"'You know what you're doing?' I ask her. 'You're talking just like the F.P. guys and Zamora: "Aw, these locals don't wanna work." Sure, most of 'em won't take the piece-rate stuff like carrots, where they only make one dollar fifty cents a day. But they want the other jobs where they get an hourly rate, even if it is only eighty-five cents. Not because they wanna work for low wages; simply because they wanna get something to eat.'

"As soon as I say that, most of the farm workers nod their heads, and Chavira turns to Rachel's partner, Eddie Perez: 'Well, what do you think we ought to do, Eddie?'

"Eddie jerks his head up with that look he gets in his eyes when he's excited: 'Strike the hell outa them!' he yells.

"'Sure,' I tell him. 'But if we don't have the jobs, who we gonna strike against?'

"'Throw a picket line around the whole damned Association,' he says. 'That'll show those bastards!'

"'Who ya gonna picket with?' I ask him. 'You haven't got the people.'

"He flips his fingers up. 'We'll get 'em.'

"'How?' I ask. 'By paying 'em to picket like you do when you go into a strike? Well, in the first place, I don't think the union's got enough money. Besides, if you start paying 'em, then that's their job; and some of 'em will want to keep picketing forever.' I look around the table: 'Anyone else have anything to say?'

"A few had. Big John had labeled the whole thing too 'pantie-waistie.' A couple of 'former farm workers' had brought up the usual 'powerful growers' crud. Finally, old Mejia really rammed it into them:

"'I guess I just don't understand,' he says. 'Here we are with a plan to help the jobless ones, and the only ones against it are the ones with jobs.' His eyes sorta jump from one of 'em to the other. 'Don't you want us to work, too? Surely, it's easy when you are working to make tremendous plans for the unemployed. "El mejor torero es él de la barrera,"' he quotes the old dicho with bitterness. 'The bravest bullfighter of all is he who has the protection of the barrier.'

"'Probably the best way,' says old man Campos, 'is for all of you to be out of work for a while and come with us every morning like Chavez does. Then maybe we'll feel more like listening to your advice.'

"'Is true,' says Chavira. 'When I first went to that F.P. office with Chavez, I was sure it would serve for nothing. But then yesterday, for the first time, I saw a look of fear in their eyes, where before it was nothing but sneering. Also, I saw Turner speak up to Zamora. Oh, not with any reckless valor, to be sure. But more than nothing as in the past. And when, I ask you, have we here in this barrio ever gotten a wire from the Governor of California, like we did tonight from Governor Brown?'

"'Brothers and sisters,' he says, stretching his arms to take us all in, 'I, for one, will keep going around and around that little path with Chavez. That's all there is to do,' he shrugs. 'Slowly, others will follow. "Poco, poquito, llena la gallina el buche."' He winks at me. 'Little by little, the chicken fills up her craw.'

"Well, what can you do against that kind of an argument, Fred? Except maybe hurry up and get on the side of the poor little guy that's out of a job. Especially when he's right there in the room watching you. Which is exactly what everybody on the C.S.O. Organizing Committee does when they vote to pass the plan, unanimously."

Chapter 9

The Turning Point

———————

The next day, everything had clicked just right for a change. It had started off with a Special Delivery letter from Carr saying he had instructed the F.P. officials to be at the C.S.O. meeting two weeks from the one they were having that same night. The Employment Committee immediately leafletted the Colonia, urging people who wanted jobs to "come to the meeting tonight and get the campaign underway." Alerted by this, the regular C.S.O. mailing, and the Telephone Committee, over five hundred people turned out.

"This time, Fred, the full resources (check that!) of the organization are put behind the Unemployed Farm Workers' Registration Drive. Every one of the 500 who come to that meeting is made a member of the Employment Committee and given a supply of 3-by-5 registration cards—white for the men, green for the women, yellow for the kids—so they can get right to work signing up the unemployed farm workers.

"And, to show 'em how important this Committee is, I tell 'em *I'll* be working fulltime for it. Also, anyone who wants a job should come to the C.S.O. office and we'll try to help them get one. But—"

"In other words, Cesar," I butted in, "instead of simply turning all that work over to the four-person Employment Committee, you harnessed the power of all the current C.S.O. members, plus all the farm workers who came to the meeting—and put that power inside the Employment Committee."

"That's right," he said.

"So the whole C.S.O. becomes the Employment Committee," I said, "focusing on that one issue, to the exclusion of everything else."

"That's true," Cesar said.

"The kind of operation," I said, "that made the C.S.O. an explosion instead of a debating society. Or a dancing club."

"Well, Fred, there's an explosion all right. A nice, big, fat one—right under me. What happens, about fifty guys show up at the office next morning looking for jobs. All the time I'm making the 'pitch' about the plan, they keep squirming around like they can hardly wait for me to finish so they can get their jobs and take off.

"But the second I get to the part about coming to the C.S.O. office and going the old F.P.-Association route with us every morning—which is really the guts of the plan and one of the main reasons we wanted to get them registered in the first place—that does it! All at once, out comes this big 'Oh-o-o-o!' from all of 'em at once, like I just rammed a red-hot poker up their behind.

"'Aw,' says one of them, 'you'll *never* get it done. (Check that 'you,' Fred.)

"'That's true,' I come back at 'em, 'but *you* and I and all of us will.'

"Then this other guy says, 'No, Chavez, we've been there before. You just can't do anything that way.' About three more guys, one after the other, say the same thing. It's their main argument. Sad to say, Fred, old Del Buono was sure right on that.

"'All right, so you've been there before,' I tell 'em. 'But you went by yourselves, didn't you? You didn't have an organization.'

"They all just shake their heads, and one of 'em says, 'Naw, the organization can't do anything on this, Chavez.' This comes from a little guy we'd just helped to get his driver's license; and I'd sort of expected that at least he would be on our side. This is when I start seeing that, with a lot of people, Fred, this business of loyalty to C.S.O. only lasts as long as they are getting the help. And I mean that one particular help, Fred—whether it's a job, or a driver's license, or name it!

"'Oh, we're wasting our time,' another one says. 'If we go with you, God knows, by the time we get back it'd be too late to even get in a little time in the carrots.' Of course this is so phony, Fred, they all have to sort of snicker, even the guy that says it.

"'Besides,' says this other guy, 'even though I know we're not gonna get a job going with you, even if we *did*, who wants to go out there to the Association at five o'clock in the morning to go to work at eight o'clock?'

"'Course, no matter what they say, Fred, I know that they'd all jump at the chance. They're just blowing off steam; and one of the most common gripes is that there's no more 'Gate Hiring' and 'Daily Pickup.' These were the things Mejia brought up that first time he came to the Hut. Remember, Fred?

"Well, about now I realize I been making the old mistake about letting 'em know how anxious *I* am to get things going. Which makes it that much easier for them to unload the whole thing on me and go about their business. So I decide to low-pressure 'em a little:

"'Sure,' I tell 'em, 'we're willing to *help* on this of the jobs. But I can't do it for you, and neither can the union. It's not *our* problem. So if you wanna go, OK. If not, well, it's still your problem.'

"Well, Fred, I thought I had had it rough at the meeting with the 'leaders,' but *this* is a stone wall. For one thing, the workers, the few that talk, have all got good arguments. Even Campos, Chavira and Mejia can't budge 'em. They aren't just blabbing to show me up either or to show off, like a lot of the 'developed leaders' do. These guys have been through it. They know. That's what makes it hard. Usually, you can get a guy to go along with you on stuff that's new to him. But when it's old to him and new to you, look out!

"Most of 'em, of course, don't say anything; but you know what that means, Fred. They don't wanna hear about some job out there in the future sometime. They want it right damn-it-snap-your-fingers *now*! So when they find out there's no jobs, and hear that you want them to do something they don't want to do, they don't argue with you or tell you they won't. They just *don't*, period. No argument!

"Anyway, I realize time's a-wasting, so pretty quick I tell 'em:

"'Well, we'll be leaving for Ventura in a few minutes. Anybody that wants to go, come on up and lemme get your name.'

"It's about like I figured it'd be. Campos, Mejia, Chavira, and a few others that went with me last week come up. The rest just sort of fade out of the office.

"Watching 'em leave, I'm really upset. Partly, I'm just plain disgusted and let down because so few of them are going with us. But then I feel a little scared, too. Because it isn't just the growers, the State, the United States Government, and C.S.O. leaders and the union I've got to contend with; now I've even got the workers going against me. Finally, I'm full of that old 'well-I'll-show-you-bastards' feeling, and I'm halfway out the door when I hear this little chuckle.

"'Mientras menos burros, más olotes,' says old Campos, chuckling again. 'The fewer the burros, the more corncobs there are for each.' That sets everybody off, even me a little. So pretty quick, with them joking, trying to cheer me up, we get into the station wagon and off we go to Ventura again, and the first stop on that lousy route from the Hut to the F.P. to the Association to the F.P. to the Association to the F.P. and on and on and on and *on* for how long, God alone knew.

"But through it all, the biggest problem, if you wanna take problems as a whole, Fred, bigger'n the fight with the F.P. and the Association, is to get the workers to go and get those damn Referral Cards. Of course, after the five of us have been at it a few days, we gradually get a few more; but after the 'raw recruits' go with us five or six times, they aren't around anymore. And it's very hard for us to go after others because, pretty quick, the five of us get so damn busy making that Rat Race, we don't have time to go and get more helpers.

"We make some headway, of course, mostly with people who can see it's a Movement, you know. I beat my lungs out explaining 'the plan' to them. At the same time, I'm afraid to go into all the little details because you never know who you're talking to.

"See, Fred, some of the 'old faithfuls' are telling me that some of the workers are spying for the Association and they want to start an investigation. I'm against this, because I just can't believe the workers would be spies. Anyway, I don't want to get all caught up in cops and robbers among ourselves and forget the main issue. But they keep after me until I finally give in and put out some bum information that on a certain date we would picket a certain grower. Sure enough, on that date there's growers' cars and State cars all over that ranch!

"Naturally, after that we had to be real careful with what we said, because if the Association knew what we were doing they would prepare themselves. We were in a real bind.

"But, as with all things, Fred, even if the Movement goes to hell, you know you'll get some people interested if you keep at it long enough."

"Some!" I laughed. "You'll get plenty, Cesar!"

"Well, we got a few anyway, and even though we didn't get any jobs we sure started learning stuff, Fred. See, one of the things we had going for us was that the Association had never faced a group that just wasn't going to give up; so they weren't prepared for us. In the past, all they had to say was, 'No jobs today.' But then we come along and say 'Why not?' So every day they are improvising, you know, giving us different answers like: 'You're not skilled enough,' or 'You're too slow,' or 'You're too fussy.' After a while, Zamora started tripping over his own lies.

"Also, hating those Referral Cards so much, I never dreamed I'd do what practically amounted to a research job on them; but that's what I start doing, Fred. I keep a record of all the cards being issued and to whom. I phone Helen at my house that so many people went to the Association today, who they are, and the numbers of the Referral Cards. (Later, when Zamora tried to say the 'locals' had not applied to him for work, we used this information against him.)

"Then there's times when the Association won't let us 'Rat Racers' into their property to hand over the cards and get turned down. So we hold onto those cards—and there were a helluva lot of 'em—and Zamora gets into trouble because he has broken the law by not collecting them from us and sending them in to the F.P. This is done on the principle of 'Hacer come hacen no es pecado,'" he chuckles. "Which means, 'Doing what is done to you is not a sin.'"

Cesar had also continued to work on Turner, sensing that, underneath, the Farm Placement representative was not such a bad guy, just scared. So while Cesar had gone on arguing with him day after day, he never antagonized Turner nor tore the place apart to impress the workers. Also, he never missed an opportunity to get inside of Turner's guard by showing appreciation for small favors and appealing to the man's compassion for the misery and degradation of the farm workers. In effect, he was treating Turner like a human being, hoping that, whenever he got the chance, Turner would deal with the workers in the same way. Cesar was "organizing" Turner.

"But this one day, Fred, while I'm really pouring it on, telling Turner how broke old Campos is, and sick and old, and how, from the F.P., I'm gonna have to take the old guy over to the Welfare Department, you know, all at once—right in the middle of this big lie—I get an idea. It's from something you told me once, Fred, and how, during the Depression, there was this outfit that put the pressure on the Welfare to get groceries for the people outa work. I start thinking, Hell! these guys here are in the same boat, practically, so why shouldn't C.S.O. put the pressure on for them?

"Soon as we leave the F.P., I take a couple of the real hard-up guys over to Welfare and start pounding on the desk. Except, instead of trying for General Relief, which is just for half-dead guys, I get 'em to apply for Aid to Needy Children on the basis they're unemployed and can't support their children. 'Course, I know Welfare won't give it to 'em; but, under the law, they have to accept their applications.

"Next I tell the Welfare that, between now and the time the State acts on the applications, these guys need General Relief. And they get it!"

It had been a classic example of "negotiation." Asking for the big one, ANC, Cesar had settled for something less. While, if he had gone for General Relief to begin with and probably been turned down, what would he have had to settle for? Exactly nothing.

"As soon as I get 'em a Grocery Order, these two guys get the message out to a few more: 'Hell! we didn't get a job, but we got something to eat!' That news really gets around, Fred. Next morning, a few more guys come to the Hut for jobs, knowing that if they don't get 'em, the least they'll get will be a Grocery Order. It's sort of a little reward, you know, for going with us."

At about the same time, there had been more excitement. The local sugar factory, where some of the C.S.O. members worked, closed down. While the workers were waiting for their unemployment insurance, they had gone with Cesar to the Association, been offered eighty-five cents-an-hour carrot jobs by Zamora and, quite naturally, refused them. The next day, they had all been dinged on the unemployment insurance claim for "refusing to accept employment!"

"Well, thanks God, Fred, this turns out to be one of those 'negatives' Alinsky talks about that's got a big 'positive' tied onto it. You see, I've got to produce for these poor guys because I got 'em into this mess. So what I do, right away I wire this hotshot in the State Department of Industrial Relations (who used to belong to the C.S.O. in L.A.) and yell for help. In nothing flat, he sends down two of his boys, we appeal the case, and zingo! we get the guys their unemployment insurance!

"Wow! Fred, when this hits the Colonia, as they say in the press, 'our stock soars!' Right away, the workers start figuring that if we could outfox the Welfare and lick the Employment Service, maybe we can take on the F.P. and the Association, too. Pretty quick, we've got a couple more carloads putt-putting along behind us on the daily Rat Race.

"Meantime, Fred, with all this stuff popping, the Unemployed Farm Workers' Registration Drive gets a real shot in the ass and the 4-by-6 cards we're using start pouring into the Hut. Housewives go door-to-door signing people up. Kids bring in the cards after school. The jobless ones drop them off all hours of the day and night."

By the end of the second week of the drive, it began to snowball. Cards began coming in from all over Ventura County: Saticoy, Camarillo, El Rio, Montalvo, Simi, Somis. Even as far away as Santa Paula, Fillmore and Piru. Then people began phoning in, from early morning until midnight, wanting to know if there were any jobs available.

"To be frank, Fred, until then I hadn't seen the unemployment thing as too big a problem. But oh my God! When the names of all those out-of-work guys start coming in, along with those phone calls, it really makes a believer out of me."

This had been the real turning point. For one thing, Cesar knew now exactly what he was in Oxnard to do. Also, on those little 4-by-6 cards he had all the proof he needed to begin blasting away at the F.P.-Association combine. Last and probably most important of all, the workers were beginning to turn to C.S.O. for jobs, which put the C.S.O. and Cesar solidly behind them in the fight. The battle lines were finally clearly drawn!

"Well, Fred, the C.S.O. mass meeting we'd been working toward begins at seven p.m. Long before that, though, I can tell by the mob streaming past me at the door, it's gonna be the biggest crowd they've ever had at Juanita School Auditorium. Word must have reached City Hall, because the cops are right on hand. Two squad cars streak down Colonia Road, slow for the traffic jam at the school, and then tear off to make the approach from the other direction. Looks like the 'City Fathers' are scared the Indians are on the warpath.

"There's a whole smear of workers coming in I've never seen before. A lot of 'em are carrying these notices we sent out (over a thousand of 'em) to all the workers we registered in the Drive. What we say in 'em, we urge 'em to come to the meeting and help us jolt the F.P. brass into (1) junking the Referral Cards, and (2) reestablishing 'Gate Hiring.'

"Anyway, by the time I've counted over six hundred of 'em pushing through the door, here comes Turner, Bates and Cunningham (Hayes' top assistant); and Del Buono starts the meeting. First, James Flores gets up and gives the grievances against the F.P. and the Association, promising the C.S.O. will fight for the rights of the workers. Then Bates comes out with a pile of bullshit which boils down to a little goat-turd, meaning that all a worker's gotta do is register with the good old F.P. and all his dreams will come true. As soon as Bates sits down, James picks up this big batch of 4-by-6 cards we registered the unemployed workers on, and yells:

"'Well, if what you say is true, Mr. Bates, how come we've got over a thousand affidavits here, signed by workers who say they can't get work?'

"'Golly, Fred! You shoulda seen the 'brass' when James said that! The three of 'em sorta start forward all at once, clear outa their chairs. Bates tries to get those cards away from James, but he won't give 'em up. If Bates wantsa look 'em over, James tells him, Bates can come down to the C.S.O. office. That way, those cards won't get 'accidentally misplaced'!

"The second James sits down, about twenty of us hit the floor at once. The 'Rat Racers' get in their two bits' worth first, practically calling Bates a liar to his face. Then Rachel, James, Soria and I take turns whaling away at 'em for making the 'locals' go clear to Ventura for Referral Cards in order to be turned down by the Association. To put a stop to that, we demand that they open an F.P. office in Oxnard, bypass the Association altogether and permit the workers to go direct to the individual growers (Gate Hiring).

"Just then, Fred, this old duck Cunningham—the 'hotshot' from Hayes' office—comes charging out, yelling he's not there to talk to James or John or me or the union crowd, but directly to the workers. The plain, honest, hard-working, God-fearing little workers. He's fully aware, he says, that all of 'em who want to work are already working, and that they are all 'good people' and don't want any trouble. Then he really starts laying it to us:

"'You're not fooling me,' he shouts, pointing his finger at James. 'I know all about those signed affidavits you say you've got. The only ones who aren't working, the ones who are stirring up all this trouble, are just a bunch of bums and winos who don't want to work, never will work, and couldn't hold a job more'n five minutes if they ever did accidentally go to work! And, by God!' he shakes his finger at the whole auditorium, 'No bunch of trash like that is gonna intimidate me!'

"Well, that's when the fun begins, Fred. This time, we don't all jump up at once, but real slow and quietlike. First, John gets up, then Rachel, then Eddie, then Campos, then James, then me. One by one, still more of us get up. At first, we all just stand there looking at the guy. After about a minute the booing begins, and a few young guys take a step toward the front.

"That does it. All at once, there goes Turner—down the stage steps, through the side door, and out. Next, Bates grabs Cunningham and drags him, drags him, Fred, still sputtering and shaking his finger at us, out the door."

After that Del Buono closed up the meeting, and he, Cesar, the Employment Committee and the union people adjourned to the Hut to live the whole thing over again. They had just started on the coffee and pan dulce (Mexican sweet bread) when the phone rang and Del Buono took it. After a minute, he put his hand over the mouthpiece and turned to Cesar:

"'It's Hayes, in Sacramento,' he whispers. 'He sounds very friendly. Says not to worry about the workers; they'll get the jobs all right, if they're qualified.'

"'Yeah, if they're qualified braceros!' I sorta bark, still pissed, I guess, at the way he'd brushed me off the last time I had talked to him. 'Look, you tell that son of a bitch if he's got anything to say to the workers, to come down here to the Employment Committee and say it!' 'Course I'm not really that mad. To tell the truth, I'm feeling pretty good about the whole thing.

"'He can't make it now.' Del Buono hangs up the phone. 'Says he's pretty busy.'

"Old man Campos grunts, 'That's Hayes, all right. He's always been too busy for us.'

"'He wasn't too busy to call us in the middle of the night.' I give him a wink. 'He never did that before, did he?' Their eyes open a little bit, and a few of them start nodding. 'It could be he's heard about tonight's meeting.'

"'So now whatta we do?' Mejia wantsa know.

"'Just keep right on doing what we're doing,' says Chavira. 'Building up our little army. We get a little strong, Hayes'll be here with us all right.'

"'Si. Al nopal lo van a ver solo cuando tiene tunas,' old Campos grins. 'As the old dicho says, "The only time they pay any attention to the cactus is when it bears fruit."'

"'That's right,' says Chavira. 'Or when we shove it up their ass!'"

Chapter 10

Getting the Goods

Two days later, when Cesar pulled up to the Hut, James Flores rushed up pointing at a picture of Hayes in the Oxnard Courier. According to the news story, Hayes was in town to install the officers of the Ventura County Farm Labor Association. The meeting would be held at the Buena Vista Camp Mess Hall.

"'What do you think we ought to do?' asks James.

"'Call the Employment Committee together,' I tell him, heading into the office.

"An hour later, Fred, the leaflet we just made begins to pop outa the mimeograph machine and into the paper holder. Across the picture of a dinky little office are the words: 'Ventura County Farm Placement Service.' Below, in the window, is a sign that says, 'Help Wanted. Braceros only. Locals, Winos and Bums need not apply.' Standing in the doorway is a likeness of Zamora, holding a puppet marked 'Hayes,' who is raising a whip at a ragged little man, who is telling him, 'But I gotta get a job, Mr. Hayes. We have no food. The rent is due. The kids are sick.'

"By four p.m. the workers have distributed five thousand of these leaflets. At six p.m., Radio Announcer Villanueva, our 'plant' at the growers' meeting, rushes into the crowd of workers at the office.

"'Man!' he flips his fingers high over his head. 'You should have been there! Braceros all around outside with their faces against the windows watching the growers eating and drinking. About halfway through Hayes' speech, a truck driver brings our leaflet to Zamora. He frowns and rushes it over to the president of the Association, who hands it to Hayes right while he's speaking.'

"'But here's the best part: Hayes looks down at the leaflet and keeps on going with the speech. All at once, he does a kind of a double take and stops and stares at that leaflet—for at least twenty seconds. Then he holds it up over his head:

"'Gentlemen,' Hayes says, and his voice is kinda shaky. "I have here in my hand a vicious little paper put out by a group that calls itself the Community Service Organization. Well, 'Disservice' would be closer to the truth. This is the kind of outfit which seeks to sow discord among our loyal farm workers—'"

"'That's right, Mr. Chavez,' says this reporter from the *Oxnard Courier*, who had just walked in. 'That's just what Hayes said. And I'd like to get a statement from you.'

"I turn to Flores, but he wants me to talk to the guy. 'We invited Hayes to meet with us,' I tell him. 'Instead, he met with the growers. This is proof of what we've suspected all along—that he's playing footsie with them. Well, we're out to break up that little game. That's why we put out that leaflet.'

"Next morning, I'm breaking in this new member, Rivera, along with Rachel and Eddie, to help us with Immigration and Citizenship cases, when a heavyset, red-faced, banker-type guy walks in: 'I'd like to speak to the person in charge,' he says.

"'You are.' I recognize him as Hayes from the Courier picture. 'Have a seat. I'll be with you in a few minutes.'

"'My time is very limited,' he says. But I'm already talking to Rivera again, so he sits down. The guys in the office seem to be getting such a kick out of it, I keep it going for about twenty minutes, watching Hayes squirm and look at his watch. Then I go up to him.

"'You wanted to see me?'

"He rises, gives me a card, which I toss on the desk: 'Hayes,' he says, 'Farm Placement.'

"'Chavez,' I say, 'C.S.O. Well, Mr. Hayes, we've been wondering when you'd show up.' I say it loud enough so that they'll all hear.

"'Yes, well I've come about this leaflet business,' he says. 'Don't you think that was a pretty irresponsible thing to do?'

"'Mr. Hayes,' I say, 'we're pretty busy around here, as you can see. So if all you want is to register a complaint, I'm gonna have to get back to these complaints Mr. Rivera and I are working on.'

"His head snaps up. 'What kind of complaints?'

"'We've got a smear of 'em. Anytime you're ready to sit down with the Committee, we'll tell you all about 'em.'

"'Well, yes,' he nods slowly. 'I think I could spare a little time.'

"'When?' I ask. 'This afternoon?'

"'I think I can arrange it,' he says.

"'OK,' I tell him. 'See you at the City Recreation Hall at four p.m.'

"'Wow!' says Rachel, when Hayes has gone. 'I don't know how in hell we did it.'

"'Why?' I ask her.

"'Why!' she yelps. 'The union's been trying to meet with him, I don't know how many times! And he's always managed to avoid us.'

"'Well, some of us have it,' I tell her, shining my nails on my shirt. 'And some of us don't.'

"'Get outa here!' she laughs, and invites me out to lunch. From then on, I notice that she and Eddie begin to get a little bit closer to C.S.O."

That afternoon, more than four hundred workers swarmed over the park surrounding the Recreation Hall. Each of them had a copy of the leaflet Cesar had gotten out that morning, showing a husky C.S.O. shoving a scared, chubby little Hayes into a meeting hall. Every few minutes, Villanueva spoke to the workers through a loudspeaker, giving them a replay in Spanish of what was going on inside the hall.

"I can hear bits of what he's saying, Fred, and he's making it sound pretty good. But we're not really prepared. Mostly, it's just a chance to let the workers sound off. Some of them are way out in left field, of course. But what's bad is Rachel and Eddie butting in all the time to talk about wages, which Hayes can't do a damn thing about.

"Pretty quick, Hayes has had enough. 'But these are just general charges,' he says. 'What I've got to have are specific complaints.'

"This is what I been waiting for. 'You're gonna get 'em, Mr. Hayes,' I tell him, motioning at the five farm workers sitting against the wall. (One of 'em is Frank Martinez, Fred. I remember all about him because he's the guy the F.P. referred to forty-two jobs before he finally got hired. Each of the workers tells how the F.P. or the growers, or both, have violated the law.

"Fred, I'm gonna give you the way it went between Frank Martinez and Hayes, because the other four were just about exactly the same:

"Hayes: 'When was the first time you got a referral?'

"Martinez: 'Oh, about two or three weeks ago.'

"Hayes: 'Did you register at Farm Placement?'

"Martinez: 'Yes.'

"Hayes: 'Where did they refer you to?'

"Martinez: 'Ventura County Farm Labor Association.'

"Hayes: 'How can you be sure of that?'

"Martinez: 'Because that's where they always send me.'

"Hayes: 'How many times have they sent you there?'

"Martinez: 'Oh, about twenty times in the past three weeks.'

"Hayes: 'Twen—unh—What was the number of the Referral Card?'

"Martinez: 'I don't know.'

"Hayes: 'When was the first time you went to the Association?'

"Martinez: 'I don't know. Two weeks ago, maybe three.'

"Hayes (squirming and looking over at Bates and Turner): 'These are pretty serious charges, Mr. Chavez. Of course, the man hasn't given us all the facts we need, but I assume they're all in the written complaint. When did you file that with us?'

"'I didn't, Mr. Hayes,' I tell him. 'We've told Bates, and he never does anything. What's the use of filing?'

"'Oh, well,' he throws up his hands with a big grin. 'Unless you write this up on one of our complaint forms, with corroborative witnesses and file it with our office, it's just your word or the worker's word against the Service or the Association. Can't get anywhere that way.'

"'And no other way, with you guys,' I finally tell him, gathering up my papers. 'So if you're not going to do anything about our complaints, we might as well wind this thing up.'

"'Now wait a minute, Mr. Chavez,' Hayes says, stretching out his hand. 'You claim these people are violating the law, don't you?' I just look at him. 'Well,' he goes on, 'the law says any complaint of a violation has to be filed. If we go ahead and take action on hearsay or anything but a filed complaint, we're in violation of the law.'

"'But even if we do file,' I tell him, 'your boys are so scared of the Association they're not gonna take any action. And you know it!'

"'We'll all get copies of those complaints, Mr. Chavez. If our local people fail to follow through, they'll hear from me, pronto. Once you file, there's no question you'll get action.'

"I keep looking at him, knowing every word he's said's a lie. But how do you prove it? And, right then, I get this idea that the only way is to accumulate so much dynamite against Hayes that we blow him the hell out of the whole state system!

"'All right!' I finally tell him, 'we'll file 'em and see. If nothing happens, there's gonna be trouble.' I pick up my papers and start moving toward the door. 'And there's no question about that, either!'"

Outside, edging through the close-packed crowd, returning the smiles, hearing the murmured greetings, the yells of "Viva Chavez!" "Viva Victoria!" he had felt bad, knowing how they'd all feel when they found out that all the victory really amounted to was the agony of writing up each of their defeats. Then it had come to him that, in a way, writing up complaints was much like registering Chicanos to vote: with only a few registered, you had nothing. Get all of them organized and registered and pounding down to the polls together, and you had it made!

"Three days after that meeting, Fred, I get an application form from

F.P., cut an electrostencile to the size of the original form and run it off on mimeo paper. I take this, along with a carload of the guys, and go to the F.P. See, what I do, Fred, as I'm filling out the form for each worker, I make a carbon copy.

"That way, we've got a record that we keep from that day on. It's got the name of the worker, job capability, work experience, and the date that the form was made out. Besides that, it's got the number of the ID card and of the Referral Card.

"After we get all this information, we come back to the office to prepare ourselves. I tell the workers: 'All right, remember—we've got to get it in writing. I want you to keep your ears open for whatever Zamora says, and when he says it. I'll be with you, but I'll be involved in other things or helping another worker, so I may miss some of it.'

"Just before we go to the Association, we have this little rehearsal. Half of the workers pretend like they're applying for a job at the Association; the other half pretend they're Zamora turning 'em down. The ones who can write put it all down on paper; the others do their best to remember.

"At the Association, of course, we get turned down. So then we write the time we arrived at the Association, what transpired, and the time we left. After that, we come back to the C.S.O. office and I take each case right to the typewriter. This takes a long time and the guys don't want to wait around. So I take half of 'em and have the rest come back later.

"Before long, Fred, we've got so many cases we have to make up a Record Form on each worker. We enter the dates of the various referrals, rejections, complaints, etc. For security, we keep this at my house. Every day, I phone the information to Helen and she enters it on the worker's record.

"Next, we go back to Turner again. But now, the whole thing is changed. I'm complaining all right, but it's all very low-key; and I'm not filing any complaints yet. 'What happened, Chavez?' Turner wantsa know.

"'Nothing,' I tell him. 'We took these eight workers and Zamora wouldn't give 'em a job.'

"'None of 'em?'

"'Not one!' I'm practically sobbing, Fred. 'But I guess we'll get some more Referral Cards and keep trying. Someday these people will understand the workers are hungry and need a job.'

"Turner looks down at the floor next to his feet, shaking his head. Then he jerks his head up toward me: 'You know what I'd do, Chavez, if I were you?' I just keep watching him staring at me. Finally he says, 'If I were you, I'd file some complaints, right now!' He reaches under the counter and comes up with some forms. 'Go ahead,' he says, 'file 'em.'

"He doesn't know how close he is to being fired, Fred. See, Bates is right behind him and heard part of what Turner said.

"'What's that, Turner!' Bates barks. Wow! Fred, Turner stiffens like he just got the well-known poker you know where.

"'That's right, Mr. Bates!' I bark back at him. 'I been telling Turner to get his ass on the ball and write up some complaints!'

"'But, Turner,' says Bates, 'didn't I hear you asking Chavez to file some complaints?'

"'Hell, no! He's not asking me! I'm having a lot of trouble with him, Mr. Bates. In fact, I think we're gonna start dealing with you from now on.' (See, Fred, Turner really wants to help us in a weird sort of a way, so I'm covering for him. It also gives me a chance to play one of 'em off against the other, you know.)

"Anyway, it works, and Bates gives me the complaint forms. 'What do you think, Mr. Bates?' I ask him. 'You heard what happened. Do you think I should file a complaint?'

"'Well, that's up to you,' he says.

"'I don't think it'll do much good,' I tell him. 'But I'll think about it.' See, Fred, I don't want to file any complaints at this point. I'm writing up all these violations now for our own records. If I start writing complaints, they'll realize what we're up to and start tightening up their operations so we can't get so much on them. As long as we don't tip our hand, then, when we do file, it'll be too late for 'em to cover things up. We'll have 'em right where we want 'em!

"Three weeks later, seeing me walk into the F.P. office with only three workers in tow, Turner practically knocks his chair down getting over to the counter:

"'What's the trouble, Chavez?' He looks at me with real concern and raises his eyes over my shoulder like he's wondering what happened to the workers' army. The day before, one hundred and twenty of us marched in there for Referrals. Bates was gonna call the cops until I accused him of discrimination and threated to call Governor Brown.

"'Filing some complaints,' I tell Turner, tossing him three originals and five copies of each.

"'You're what—?' Turner kind of squeaks like he can't believe it. 'Well, where are the complainers?'

"'Right over there.' I snap my head toward the three workers leaning by the office door.

"'Oh.' His eyes keep moving from me to the workers. 'Unh-hunh!' Then he jerks around toward the desk where Bates is sitting. 'Mr. Bates, we have some complaints here against the Association.'

"'Unh-hunh.' Bates hardly looks up from the magazine he's reading. 'Well, you know the procedure.'

"'But, Mr. Bates—' Turner takes a few steps toward his boss. 'These are *filed* complaints!'

"'What's that?' Bates pops forward in the swivel chair, the magazine fluttering out of his hands. 'Are the workers registered?'

"'Yes,' says Turner. 'We have their names.'

"'Referral Cards?' Bates says. Turner nods. 'How about their ID cards?'

"'Here they are.' I pull the three cards out of my pocket. Turner gives the three complaints to Bates and leans against the wall behind him. Bates glances through the complaints, looks down, clears his throat, and moves some papers around his desk. After a minute or so, Turner leans down close to his boss, almost whispering, 'Maybe you better call the Association, uh?'

"'Go ahead,' Bates mutters. Straightening up like he just smelled some cat shit, Turner gives a big sigh and slumps into a chair by the phone and dials.

"He puts his hand over the mouthpiece and looks at me: 'Still the low man on the totem pole around he—Oh, Mr. Zamora?' He starts forward. 'Turner, Farm Placement.' Now smiling into the phone, he turns away, murmuring. But I hear enough sweet talk to be able to make a pretty close guess how far we're gonna get with our complaints.

"'Hey, Chavez.' He gives me this fake frown. 'Mr. Zamora says these men turned down those jobs.'

"'Unh-hunh,' I nod. 'And I saw Zamora turn these men down. And so did three other witnesses. So now what are you gonna do?' Just then the three workers come up and stand beside me.

"'What can we do?' Bates comes over next to Turner. 'It's just your word against theirs.' The four of us stand there with our arms folded, looking at the two of them.

"Finally, Bates throws up his hands. 'Well, that's about all we can do, I guess.' And he starts back toward his desk.

"'We're not playing any guessing games today!' I yell after him. 'You aren't gonna fluff us off with a lotta malarky this time, Bates. I filed some complaints and the rules say you've got to investigate 'em and send 'em up to your boss in Sacramento.'

"At the last word, he whirls around. 'I know my rules,' he growls.

"'Sure,' I nod. 'But have you got the guts to enforce 'em?'

"'We'll see.' He goes back to his desk as we walk out.

"On the way back to Oxnard, Angel grins. 'Man, you sure told that guy!' I don't say anything. I'm looking straight ahead through the windshield, trying to hide the mad, scared, beat feeling, when Chavira opens it up:

"'Yeah, but whatsa use kidding ourselves? It ain't gonna do no good.'

"'I wouldn't say that.' I give him a quick look through the rear-view mirror.

"'We gotta get proofs, compadre.' Angel's head goes around toward Chavira in the back seat. 'Remember our plan?'

"'Proofs!' grunts Chavira. 'Those guys know what's going on.'

"I know just how the poor guy feels. He's got no job. There's no money coming in. He's worrying about his family. He's catching hell from his wife, the grocer, and everybody else he owes. On top of that, he's figuring we're using him in some weird plan that he's almost positive will fail. But, counting heavily on that 'almost' part, I go after him like I've been doing with all the rest for weeks:

"'Look, Chavira, before I came here I didn't know things were this bad with the "locals." But you and the other guys told me and then I saw it myself. Now I know, and C.S.O. knows too. But does Governor Brown know? Does Carr, the boss of that no-good Hayes, know? And how about the Federal guys?'

"There's not a sound from the back seat, so I go on. 'We got the goods on Zamora, didn't we? And we just filed 'em, didn't we? That's the first step. Now we wait. If the F.P. moves, OK. If not, we'll have the proof they're playing footsie with the growers. And then, by God, we'll throw the force of the whole C.S.O. Movement—and all the Chicano voters in California—against the Brown Administration. We'll blow this thing sky-high!'

"A few days later, I'm in the F.P. office with about fifty workers for Referral Cards. While I'm waiting, I file seventy-five more complaints and check with Bates on what he's done on the fifty we filed last week.

"'They're no good, Chavez,' he kinda snarls. 'They have to be in the worker's own handwriting.'

"God, I'm so damn mad, it's all I can do to keep from slugging him. You see what's happening, Fred? They aren't just dragging their feet; that's to be expected. What they're doing, they're telling me and the workers, 'Go ahead. You've gone the old Rat Race for forty days, go forty more. You followed the rules. You gathered all the proof against us. So shove it!'

"'You understand what he said?' I ask the workers. They're all crowding around me, nodding and muttering. 'OK,' I push through them toward the door. 'Let's get out of here!'

"Even before we get outside, Big John starts grousing. 'Never get nowhere this way. Gotta stand up to those SOBs! Fight 'em.'

"I lead all the workers across the street where my car is, tear off a complaint against Bates, and get 'em all to sign it. Then I take 'em all back into the F.P. office and throw the complaint on the counter. 'There's one against you, Bates!' I yell at him. 'All in my own handwriting!' I don't even wait for an answer. I just keep moving, leading 'em out the door, and up the street to the cars.

"Back at the C.S.O. office, while Angel is calling the Employment Committee together, I get Carr on the line and tell him about Bates and the complaints.

"Who's paying for this call, Mr. Chavez?' he wantsa know.

"'We are,' I tell him. 'And we can't afford it, either.'

"'Reverse the charges,' he says. 'And hold on a minute.'

"Pretty quick he's back. 'Mr. Chavez. I've contacted Ventura Farm Placement and they tell me they have no knowledge of those complaints.'

"'They what!' I yell into the phone. 'Now look, Mr. Carr, I've got at least ten witnesses right here by the phone that saw me file 'em. Not only that, but I've got copies of all the seventy-five others we filed in the past week, along with the one I filed against Bates. Want me to send 'em up to you?'

"'Hold them,' he says. 'I'll look at them down there.'

"'When are you coming?' I ask him.

"'Oh, one of these days,' he says, and hangs up.

"Well, with nothing more encouraging than that, it's hard telling the guys. But they take it pretty good, most of 'em. 'Course, John and Rachel and Eddie look kinda down. And later, some of the workers tell me they think we're going too slow on the employment thing."

Chapter 11

Making Contact with the Enemy

"One morning a few days later, some guy that looks like a banker comes swinging into the office. He's very well-dressed and the first thing that hits my mind is, Oh-oh, here comes a rat!

"'Mr. Chavez?' he asks. I nod. 'Carr, Employment Service.' Immediately I know I've misjudged him. Even in those first few words, I get the feeling he's interested, you know. Genuinely concerned about the problem.

"'I'd like to see those complaints,' he says. 'Any place I can get off by myself and look 'em over?' I take him back to the little room in the rear and give him the complaints. In about an hour he comes out:

"'Nobody but you knows I'm here today, Mr. Chavez. And that's the way I want it.' Carr thumbs through the stack of complaints. 'I'm pretty green on all this stuff. So far I've just heard the growers' point of view. Now I wanna learn about the worker. Like to talk to some of 'em, see how they live, where they work, etc. Could you take me around?'"

For the rest of the day with Cesar, Carr listened to the words of the workers in their homes, in the fields, the camps, the cantinas. Often, their thoughts had come out slowly and after much patient prompting by Cesar. Sometimes they came in a rush, like a stream that's been clogged and suddenly cleared. But slow or fast, the words all told one thing: the story of grower-F.P. collusion to eliminate the "locals." And all through the day, at every opportunity, Cesar had rammed home the point that the only solution lay in a thorough housecleaning inside the Farm Placement Service, beginning with Mr. Hayes!

"About a week later, Carr phones: 'What's happening down there?' he wantsa know.

"'Filed about one hundred more complaints,' I tell him.

"For a few seconds, there's just silence at his end. Then in this very low voice, he says, 'Any action?'

"'Naw,' I tell him. 'Same old crap. Your guys down here are still checking with the Association. Zamora's denying our charges. And that's as far as it goes.'

"'How come you haven't been sending me my copy, Chavez?'

"'Whataya mean?' I start forward. 'We been mailing you copies of every damn one of 'em.' Then somewhere in my head the old neons ping on: 'Hey, maybe I better send 'em registered after this, uh?'

"'Better'n that,' he says, giving me another address. 'Send 'em there. It's my home.' He rings off.

"In about a week, here comes a note from Carr: 'I'm getting them; keep it up,' it says. But nothing happens. Nothing but the same old F.P.-Association runaround, and the workers griping louder, and Big John, Rachel and Eddie still giving the whole idea the big razz-berry because we aren't producing.

"One morning about a week later, I'm there at the F.P. complaining to Turner as usual—not because I expect any action, you know, just to build up my case—when the phone rings and Turner answers it. After a second or two, I hear him say, 'Oh, sure. How many? Twenty braceros, uh? Sure, we'll get 'em for you. Right, the Association. Yamato Ranch in Oxnard, uh? Jumbo carrots, yeah. Topping, OK. Twelve cents a sack, uh? Where you calling from? Soledad, uh? And what's your name again? Ledesma. OK, Mr. Ledesma. See you tomorrow.'

"Well, Fred, all during that conversation my little rabbit ears are flapping frantically. In the first place, 'topping' jumbo carrots (as opposed to 'tying' ordinary carrots) is fast, and it pays four cents more a sack. It's a pretty good job. And Ledesma, the contractor, is a pretty good guy. Remember him, Fred, in the Soledad C.S.O.?

"So the second Turner hangs up, I say, 'Look, Turner, this guy's contracting carrots. And we've got a helluva lot of people out of work. We want those jobs!'

"'But this guy wants the workers tomorrow,' says Turner.

"'Turner, we've *got* the workers. Right now!'

"'Gee, I'd like to,' he says, 'but I have to talk to Bates.'

"'Bates, nothing!' I yell, starting out the door. 'You just talk to Ledesma. Tell him we'll see him at Yamato's Ranch in the morning!'

"But I'm not taking any chances, Fred. Chavira waits at the F.P. for Ledesma and gets him to call me. I put it to him straight about the carrots: 'There's gonna be some jobs for the "locals" out there, isn't there?' I ask him.

"'It's possible,' he says. 'But we're gonna work the braceros.'

"'Look,' I tell him. 'There's a lot of people out of work around here, and we'd like to get those jobs.'

"'But, Chavez,' he says, 'the "locals" aren't dependable.'

That's how it is now.

"You know, we skipped the Association when we got this job,' I tell 'em. 'So what's to keep us from doing it again? Just bypass the Association and go directly to the individual grower-members. If they've got braceros, they fire 'em and hire you folks.'

"Driving back, I start wondering just how far we're gonna be able to get with that idea. Isn't that the reason the F.P. and the Association joined together in the first place—to make sure that kinda stuff never happens? But just then, Fred, this other idea pings: Whatta we got to lose? Besides, even if we lose, it's just one thing more we can write up to get Carr off his ass and pushing hard on those complaints of ours. Actually, it's one of those rare cases where you can't lose for winning.

"That same night, Fred, we thrash the idea out with the Employment Committee, and they're all hot for it. The hard part, they figure, is gonna be finding out about the good jobs in advance so we can throw the 'locals' in there fast before the braceros finish up the job. I'm still worrying about this later over a beer at the Coconito Bar.

"The Coconito is jumping with braceros. Two of 'em, I notice, are talking to Nellie Gutierrez, one of the barmaids, who has a soft spot for C.S.O. because we helped her beat a phony hooker rap. Pretty quick she comes over to take our order. Nellie is what they used to call 'pleasingly plump' like all the barmaids are from having to drink so much beer on the job. (The ladies in the barrio have a cruel name for them— 'los hippos.') And she has this beautiful, long, purple-scarlet dress on. While I'm looking at her, this idea hits: 'Hey, Nellie,' I smile up at her, 'you remember what you told me the last time you were over at the office?'

"'Sure do,' she nods, hitting this hip-shot stance.

"'OK!' I signal her over close. 'We need that help right now.'

"'How?' Nellie leans down toward me.

"'Well, you girls know the braceros pretty well, don't you?'

"'Hm,' she shrugs. 'Well enough, I guess.'

"'Well enough to find out where they work?'

"'Ha!' she laughs. 'That's easy. They're always bragging about those good jobs they're holding down.' Her eyes wander over to the braceros at the bar and then jump back to mine. 'You know what, Mr. Chavez? I bet I could even get their numbers for you if you want.'

"'Yeah?' I snap to attention, thinking, Christ! this woman's way ahead of me. 'How could you do that?'

"'I'll show you.' She serves our beer and then goes back to the braceros she was talking to when we came in. Pretty quick, I see 'em reach for their wallets, open 'em up, and hand 'em to Nellie. In a while she comes back and gives us their numbers.

"'Well, I'll be!' I shake my head. 'How'd you swing it?'

"'Easy,' she laughs. 'I just ask them if they have a snapshot of themselves, and they pull out their contract papers with their numbers up at the top.'

"'Listen, Nellie,' I motion her down close again. 'You think you might be able to get some of the other girls from the other joints together for a little meeting tomorrow?'

"'Oh, sure.' She snaps her fingers. 'That's even easier. Gang of us girls have breakfast together every noontime at the Blue Onion.'

"And Fred, that's how the Oxnard Barflies Committee was born.

"Two nights later, I'm there at the office at about eleven o'clock talking to Employment Committee Chairman James Flores, when the phone rings. It's Nellie Gutierrez, recently elected head of the Barflies Committee:

"'Hey, Mr. Chavez!' She comes on all excited. 'Look, I got a hot tip right now. There's thirteen of 'em working at Jones' Ranch, right by the road.'

"'Swell, Nellie!' I'm practically panting. 'What in?'

"'Tomato seedlings,' she whispers. 'You want their numbers?' I write 'em down and hang up, turning to James Flores:

"'Let's go!' I start for the door.

"'Where to?' He follows me.

"'Braceros at Jones' Ranch.' We get in the car. 'Gotta line up a crew of "locals" tonight and go after those jobs.'

"Next morning, we're all up at the F.P. office crowding around Turner as he finishes talking to Zamora on the phone. 'There's no work at Jones' place,' he says, turning to me. 'Zamora said—'

"'I don't give a damn what Zamora said!' I bust in. 'We just came from there. There's a crew of braceros working the seedlings, and we want those jobs!'

"'Calm down, Chavez.' Turner raises his hands like he's trying to protect himself. 'You say one thing, Zamora says something different, and I haven't time to go out there—!'

"'Look, Turner.' I bend over toward him. 'This is one time we're not gonna get screwed by you and Zamora! We got the numbers of every damn one of those braceros.' His mouth kinda drops open as I go on: 'So there is not gonna be any of this "your word against his" shit. Now do we get those jobs, or do we have to go "upstairs"?'

"'Wait, Chavez.' His hands come up like he's pushing us away from him. 'I can refer these workers out to the Association all right, and if Zamora—'

"'Not this time, Turner.' I nip him off. 'We want 'em direct to Jones. Just like you sent 'em direct to Yamato's place when Ledesma came down here for the carrots.' For a second his eyes twitch back and forth like he doesn't know which way to jump and wishes Bates was here to make the decision for him. Then he takes a big breath and throws up his hands:

"'OK,' he says. 'We'll sign 'em up. But it isn't going to work.'

"Now, heading for Jones' Ranch, the workers all souped up joking about how far they're gonna throw those braceros' asses out of there, I start worrying. Never figuring we'd get through F.P. that easy, we hadn't planned the next move. All I know, for sure, is we can't have any rough stuff. I'm just starting to warn 'em on this when we reach Jones' Ranch and spot the braceros. I park by the side of the road and we all go scrambling over the irrigation ditch and onto the property.

"The second we hit the field, the action begins. The braceros see us and stop work. Old man Martinez, Jones' foreman, comes out of the barn and up to us.

"'Mr. Jones here?' I ask him.

"He shakes his head. 'Qué le pasa?' he asks. 'What's going on?'

"'These men want to work.' I hand him the Referral Cards.

"'How many?' he asks.

"'Thirteen.'

"I walk over to the braceros. 'We have nothing against you guys,' I tell 'em. 'But these men with me are all local workers, and—'

"'Sí, sí. Ustedes tienen derecho,' one says. 'Surely, it is your right.' Then, smiling good-naturedly, they all walk past me, hand their hoes to the 'locals,' and head for the barn. Old man Martinez follows them, while I thin out a few tomatoes to see if I still remember how."

Cesar had remembered, all right. The memory of the last time he had used the short-handled hoe in Oxnard was suddenly with him, joining the exhilaration that had just come when the braceros "surrendered" their arms to the victorious "local" army! That was a good one, he sneered to himself. Hell! they hadn't even made contact with the real enemy yet!

"Lucky for me I stuck around, Fred. Before long, here comes the old foreman galloping out of the barn, the braceros dawdling in a bunch behind him. Uh-oh, I say to myself, here we go!

"'Listen!' The old man comes up to me breathing hard. 'Zamora says no work! He himself will be here soon.' He puts out his hand: 'The hoes, please.'

"I nod at the 'locals' and toss the old guy my hoe, thinking: No use arguing with him, but we gotta do something real fast. One by one, some shrugging, others cussing softly, the 'locals' toss their hoes to the ground and watch the braceros pick them up and go back to work in the seedlings.

"That's all I been waiting for. 'Wait here,' I tell our guys, heading for my car.

"'What now, Chavez?' one of 'em calls after me with bitterness. 'Back to the office to put it in the little writing-machine again?'

"'No,' I shake my head, 'into the telephone. And we're gonna go clear to the President of the United States, if we have to!'

"Back at the office, I get on the phone, and the old buck-passing begins.

Bates won't move on the thing until he talks to Morales. Morales won't move until he talks to his boss, Crittendon, in Los Angeles. Who won't move until he checks with his Washington office.

"'Forget it, Crittendon!' I yell into the phone. 'Just give me the Secretary of Labor's number!' After a long silence, he says, 'OK, Chavez, you win. How do I get to the Jones Ranch?'

"I just get back to the ranch when Zamora's big, black Cadillac zooms up with the Sheriff right behind him. Jumping out of his car before it's completely stopped, the Sheriff swaggers over to me: 'Is this the man?' he asks Zamora.

"Zamora scrambles out of the Cad. 'That's him, Sheriff. He's the one that's causing all the trouble. Him and that damned C.S.O. outfit!'

"'C.S.O.?' The Sheriff's head jerks around toward Zamora, and his voice goes down. 'I thought you said C.I.O.'

"'What's the diff?' Zamora sneers. 'We want him and the rest of 'em off this property, right now!'

"The Sheriff gives me a friendly grin and turns to Zamora. 'I think we can settle this without anybody getting all steamed up about it. Now then, Mr.—unh?'

"'Chavez,' I shoot back. 'With C.S.O.'

"'Oh, yes.' His head bounces up and down and he shakes hands with me. 'Been hearing a lot of good things lately about your group, Mr. Chavez. Certainly did a fine job getting all those folks out to vote.'

"'That's right, Sheriff,' I look around at the 'locals.' 'And now we're trying to get 'em all out to work.'

"'Fine, fine.' He smiles, rubbing his hands. 'And I'm sure you will, too.' Then his face hardens up a little. 'We just gotta be a little more careful about how we go about doing it, don't we?' I keep looking at him, and he starts smiling again: 'Best thing you can do is take the folks off Mr. Jones' property. That way there won't be no trouble about trespassin', and everything'll be OK, uh?'

"I point my head toward the road: 'Anything wrong with just sitting out in the car?'

"'No. Not as long as you don't make no trouble.' Then he squints his eye: 'But what for, Mr. Chavez?'

"'We wanna wait for Jones.' I start for the car, motioning to the guys. 'How'd you like that Mr. Chavez? See what a few votes'll do?' They chuckle, and I give 'em the dope about Crittendon, while we all sit there watching Zamora and the Sheriff watching us. Then the Sheriff leaves and Zamora goes over and gets in his Cad. Just then a car roars up and Rachel jumps out, yelling:

"'What are you guys waiting for, Cesar?' Her head jerks toward the braceros. 'You gonna let those guys steal your jobs? Come on—'

"'Slow down, Rachel,' I cut in on her. 'We're going in all right, but not that way.' I give her a quick fill-in on how we stand.

"'What do we have to wait for Crittendon for? We can throw them out ourselves.' I shake my head.

"'Vengase! muchachos!' she yells to the workers. 'Come on, boys!' Nobody moves. But Zamora jumps out of his Cad and yells something at Rachel.

"Then things really start popping. Just as Rachel and Zamora are tearing toward each other, another car slides in behind me and Crittendon, this real tall, lanky blond guy, gets out. I'm introducing him to all the workers when the Sheriff rolls up and Zamora comes rushing over toward us:

"'All right, Sheriff, you seen it yourself this time. Now, no more monkey business! Take these guys in!'

"Crittendon steps out in front of us. 'There's a labor dispute here, Sheriff.'

"'Wait a minute!' Zamora squirms in between the government guy and the Law. 'Who are you?'

"'Department of Labor.' Crittendon hands Zamora and the Sheriff his card.

"'Zamora, Ventura County Grow—uh, Farm Labor Association,' the bracero-herder mutters. "But there's no labor dispute here, Crittendon. These guys are trespassing on Jones' property. If they want jobs, they have to come to the Association like everybody else. They know that. They're just a buncha damn troublemakers, that's all!'

"'Look, Zamora,' Crittendon interrupts, 'Farm Placement referred these men here. So if anyone's making trouble, it's you, not the—'

"'Hey!' Some tall guy in a Texas hat and boots gets out of a car that just came up and stomps over through the workers. 'What's goin' on here?'

"Zamora points at Rachel and me. 'Those two are raising hell with the braceros, Mr. Jones!'

"'Look, you.' Jones swings around and starts toward me, red-eyed mad. 'You get the hell off my property or I'll kill—'

"'Hold it!' Crittendon yells, barring the grower's way. 'I wouldn't do that if I were you, Jones. You'll just make it tough on yourself and the Association.'

"Jones' head snaps back: 'Who are you?'

"Crittendon flips open his wallet with his credentials. 'You better slow down, Jones. You're already in violation of the law, replacing domestic workers with braceros.'

"'Hey,' Jones looks around at Zamora. 'What's going on around here? You told me we didn't have to worry about these guys.' He points his head toward Crittendon.

"'Well, never mind.' Zamora looks down at his feet. 'We'll take it up at the next meeting of the Association.'

"'I don't know.' Crittendon shakes his head slowly. 'That may be too late.'

"'What does that mean?' Jones takes off his big hat and wipes the sweat off his forehead.

"'Don't you know you can lose your braceros for good for what you've done?'

"'Hey now, hold on,' Jones kinda groans, twisting his hat in his big hands. Watching him, the workers' eyes light up. 'Gosh, Mr. Crittendon,' he says, 'I didn't know about all them rules.'

"'Well, here it is.' Crittendon opens the book and hands it to Jones. 'Right there in the contract you signed with the government.' The grower looks at it fast and hands it back.

"'Yeah, I guess so.' Jones looks down, kicking the dirt with his boot. 'But nothing like that ever happened before. The Association just—'

"'Never mind that.' Crittendon looks hard at Zamora. 'I'll get to the Association later. What I'm interested in right now is whether you're going to pull those Nationals out of there and put these "locals" to work, or am I gonna have to—'

"'Oh, sure, sure.' Jones' hand comes up as though he's ready to take an oath. 'I'm not looking for no trouble around here a-tall. Uh, Juan,' he calls old man Martinez. 'Take 'em to the barn, and put these folks to work.'

"This time, Fred, I figure we really nailed it down. And I sorta float back to town on the wings of victory!

"At the C.S.O. office a while later, Crittendon flips through this foot-high stack of complaints we've accumulated. 'This is really something!' he says. 'How long did it take you?'

"'Bout two months,' I tell him.

"'And Hayes and his boys haven't acted on a single damn one of 'em, unh?'

"I'm just starting to take off on Hayes, when this guy, Gomez, comes in. He's one of the Commandos we organized that afternoon to 'reconnoiter bracero emplacements.' (How do you like that one, Fred?)

"'How did it go?' I ask Gomez.

"'I almost got caught,' he chuckles, slouching down on the desk. 'See, I was there in Somis Camp, Cesar, telling the braceros why we had to bump those guys today at the Jones Ranch and, all at once, some guy yells, "Callete! Callete! The dispatcher's coming!" My God! Cesar, I ain't got time to run, so I just jump into one of the braceros' bunks and yank the covers over my head.' Gomez shakes his head, laughing. 'Those braceros got a big charge out of it.'

"'How'd they like the leaflets?' I ask Gomez. (See, Fred, we'd run off this leaflet, explaining C.S.O.'s program to the braceros.)

"'Oh, fine,' our Commando nods. ''Specially the part about how C.S.O. will try to help the braceros at the Service Center. That reminds me, Cesar, I ran into one of Jones' braceros and he was pretty worried. Says Zamora's sending them all out there again tomorrow.'

"I look over at Crittendon real fast. 'Probably thinks you've gone back to L.A. already.'

"'Well, we'll just fool that little man.' He grabs the phone and reserves a room at a motel.

"By six a.m. Crittendon, the workers, and I are all out at the Jones Ranch. No one's around but old man Martinez.

"'No work today,' he says.

"'When'll you start?' I ask.

"'Quién sabe?' he shrugs. 'Who knows?'

"We're not buying that. We leave James Flores to keep an eye on the ranch and the rest of us go over to my place, which is close by, for some coffee. We're just having our second cup when James comes skidding into my front yard.

"'They're there, all right!' he hollers. 'Way over behind the house so you can't see 'em from the road.'

"As soon as we get back to the ranch, the braceros walk off the job. Jones, looking real gone, comes out and puts our guys to work. Crittendon just stands there, writing in his book. Finally, he flips it shut and turns to the grower:

"'If you're smart, Jones, you'll hold on to those domestics.'

"'I know,' Jones shakes his head. 'I tried to tell Zamora . . .'

"'Because, if I have my way,' Crittendon butts in, 'you're going to be decertified.'

"Jones still stands there shaking his head and I'm on this little cautious, halfway 'high' as we pull off for town.

"Back at the C.S.O. office, I ask Crittendon, 'What do you mean by that "decertify" stuff?'

"Crittendon looks up from where he's typing up the complaint: 'Bar him from getting any more Nationals.'

"'That's what I thought,' I tell him. 'But what about all those complaints we filed against the Association? They're the ones that oughta be decertified.'

"Crittendon shrugs. 'I can't help you there. That's up to Farm Placement.' I guess I musta looked pretty beat.

"'Cheer up, Chavez,' he kinda snickers. 'I have a hunch that as soon as Carr hears about my decertification complaint on Jones, things are really going to start popping.'

"'How soon'll that be?' I ask him.

"'Oh, maybe a week or two,' he says, settling back to his typing.

"But hell, Fred, we can't wait that long! About a minute later, I'm on the phone spilling the whole thing to Carr in Sacramento. When I'm through he talks to Crittendon and then gets me on again.

"'Listen, Chavez,' he says. 'I been holding off on this complaint deal until I got the right kind of a pretext to move in. This Jones thing looks like it. Hayes is on vacation, so I'm coming down there myself.'

"'How soon?' I wanna know.

"'You'll hear from me in a week. OK?' He rings off."

Chapter 12

The Battle Roars On

———

"A few days later, Carr comes to town, and this time it's no secret. He calls everybody together—Turner, Bates, Morales, Crittendon, the union, and C.S.O.—and starts right in on the complaints:

"'Understand some of the C.S.O. members have filed complaints with our local office.' He looks at me, and I look at James Flores.

"'That's right, Mr. Carr.' James sets two big soap boxes jammed with Complaints in front of Carr.

"'What's this?' Carr looks up at him.

"'Complaints,' says James. 'Against the Association.'

"'All those?' Carr holds his hands out toward the boxes. James nods. 'Well, but my God!' (Carr's really putting on an act, Fred.) 'How many have you got there?'

"'Around fourteen hundred,' says James. 'And that's not counting the ones we've filed against the Farm Placement for—'

"'Fourteen hundred!' Carr squeals. 'How many workers are involved?'

"'What'd we figure?' James looks at me. 'Around four hundred, wasn't it, Cesar?' I nod. 'And that's not counting—'

"'I know,' says Carr. 'That's not counting the ones you filed against Farm Placement for sitting on their behinds!' Carr swings toward Bates: 'Why hasn't my office received copies of these, according to instructions?'

"Bates wobbles his head from one side to the other. 'Well, uh, we had intended sending them in, Mr. Carr, but many of them were not legitimate complaints. And Mr. Hayes—'

"'Mr. Bates!' Carr's hand slams down on the table. 'I don't give a—' He stops himself, looks down, and takes a deep breath. 'Mr. Bates—' His voice is low and very tight. 'After this, you send me a copy of every one of those complaints, good, bad or indifferent!' Bates nods.

"'Now then.' Carr looks from Bates to the boxes in front of him. 'What action have you taken on these?'

"'Well,' Bates clears his throat. 'We checked with the Association, and they denied the charges.'

"Carr cocks his head back. 'In other words, if the Association denies it, that's proof there's nothing there, right?' Bates nods. 'So nothing further was done, uh, Bates?'

"Bates starts to speak, but right then Rachel cuts in: 'Yes, and every time we go to his office, they treat us like dirt!' Oh, Christ! I start thinking, here we go again. "'Mr. Chavez.' Carr snaps me back to the meeting. 'Has this been your experience, too?'

"'If they don't crowd me, I don't get on them,' I tell Carr. "'But I'd like to get back to what we were talking about before. The only reason we went to all this work on these complaints is because Hayes told us that was the only way we could ever get any action. So we filed 'em, and that's the last we ever heard about 'em.

"Carr looks at Bates again. 'Don't you ever tell the workers the disposition of their cases?'

"'Sometimes.' Bates' voice is real low.

"'That's a lie, Mr. Bates!' yells Eddie. 'And you know it!'

"'What about it, Mr. Chavez?' says Carr. (He seems to trust me more now, Fred, after what I just said.)

"'Well,' I shake my head. 'I never heard him tell anyone. And I've been taking the workers to the Farm Placement office every morning for the last two months.'

"'What's that?' Carr jerks around toward Bates. 'Is that true?' Bates nods. 'And how many of them have you referred, Bates?'

"'Oh,' Bates screws up his mouth. 'Between four and five hundred.'

"'Uh-huh,' says Carr. 'And how many have been placed on jobs?'

"'Well,' Bates gives him a sort of jittery little grin. 'I can't tell you exactly, but—'

"'I can,' I cut in. 'Thirty-four at Yamato's place, and thirteen at Jones Ranch.

"'Uh-huh,' says Carr, nodding his head. 'That's forty-seven. Now, how many Nationals are working around here?'

"'Oh.' I threw up my hands. 'Thousands!'

"I hardly get the words out before Carr explodes all over Bates: 'Are you trying to tell me, Bates, that with thousands of Nationals working and with Mr. Chavez, here, going to all the trouble of bringing domestic workers to you—not just sending them, hoping they get there, but actually delivering them right to your doorstep—are you trying to tell me that all you could place was a measly forty-seven of them?'

"'Well, we try,' says Bates, putting his hands out toward Carr. 'But the Association says that these men won't work, and so—'

"Carr's hand hits the top of the table: 'I don't give a damn what the Association or anyone else says! This monkey business has got to stop! From now on, I want your office and the Federal people to make a personal investigation of every single complaint you get, and check with each other on it!'

"'That's fine with me,' says Crittendon. 'And if your people won't move, is it OK if we go it alone?'

"'You bet it is!' Carr jerks his head down hard. 'Just one thing, though,' he says, and a quick little grin jumps out of his eyes. 'If that ever happens, I want to know about it.'

"Then his eyes get serious again, and he looks around the table and stops at me. 'All right, what else have you got on your mind, Mr. Chavez?'

"For the next hour, we go into the other stuff we need: Gate-hiring, worker pickup by the grower at the C.S.O. office, establishment of an F.P. office in Oxnard, etc. But since Carr's green on all these things, he says he'll send Hayes down in a few days to thrash it out with us. I guess he can tell I'm not so hot for this because, when we break up, he gives me the high sign to follow him.

"Soon as we're outside, he shakes his head: 'Something rotten in my Department, Mr. Chavez.' I just keep walking, waiting. When we get to his car, he leans on the top, looking down. 'Gotta figure some way to clean it up.' He gets in and starts the car, and sticks his head back out. 'Now, when you meet with him—'

"'Who?' I ask.

"'Huh?' He seems surprised. 'Oh, I'm sorry. Hayes.' I look away.

"'What's the matter, Cesar?' (Check that, Fred, *Cesar*.)

"I shake my head. 'We've been that road before.' (I'm giving him the same thing the workers gave me, Fred, that time I tried to get 'em in the Rat Race, remember?)

"Carr gives me that little eye-grin again. 'I think you'll find it a little different this time.'

"'It'll never be any different,' I tell him. 'As long as he's in there. Why, hell! Mr. Carr, he's working for the growers! Everybody knows that. So why don't you fire him and let the guys he's working for pay his salary!'

"He flashes a smile and starts the motor. 'Listen, Cesar, I'm gonna talk to you just before that meeting. Then I want you to call me back as soon as it's over and let me know if you've made any progress.' He starts to back out of the parking lot. 'And none of this hocus-pocus stuff this time. You know what you need, so bear down on him. OK?' He straightens his wheels. 'And be sure you keep Crittendon busy on those complaints, uh?'

He waves and drives away.

"Well, I don't like it, Fred. But I have to shove it on the back burner because the next day, Nellie, the Queen of the Barflies, gives us the word the flowers are beginning. Hell! that's the best-paying job in the valley, Fred; and the women are really good at it. So all day long, we rush them up to the F.P. to get referred to the flowers, nothing but flowers!

"Next morning, of course, we're up there in front of Zamora and he's pissed: 'Hey, what's going on here?' he growls, thumbing through the Referral Cards of the 'locals.' 'You guys trying to get a monopoly on the flowers or something?' We all just keep looking at him. 'OK,' he kinda sneers, 'let's go.'

"I stand there watching the women pile in the truck from the Williams Flower Ranch thinking: Hey, it worked better'n we thought it would, didn't it. Well, maybe so, I say to myself; but it's just another battle and the war roars on. Yeah, and more than likely, it's another skirmish, and the battle roars on.

"That's how it turns out, Fred. Next morning, Zamora goes 'underground.' When the women show up at Williams' place, there's no work for 'em. The old foreman meets 'em at the gate and tells 'em a crew of braceros came real early, cut all the flowers, and took off.

"It's Zamora all right, trying to mow us down with speed and numbers.

"When the women get back to the C.S.O. office, James, Campos, Angel and some of the other farm workers are there and the phone is ringing. I grab it.

"'Chavez?' comes the voice. 'Jones. Look, tomatoes are coming fast. Got anymore people around there want to work?'

"'Sure have, Mr. Jones.' I yell it out so the workers'll all hear me. 'How many?'

"'Least twenty-five,' he says.

"'Yeah, I think we can get 'em,' I tell him. 'Be a while, though. They've all got Referrals to the flowers. Have to get 'em new cards at the Farm Placement and take 'em over to Zamora—'

"'Hell with that!' he breaks in. 'I need them guys now, not next week. You just hold 'em there. I'll send the truck down right away.'

"I turn from the phone and give the guys the scoop. 'You know what that means?' I smile around at 'em.

"'Sure,' says Angel. 'It's like it was in the days before the Association. We skip Zamora and get hired right at the grower's gate.'

"'And they pick us up,' says Campos, 'as of old.'

"'Even better than that,' I grin at 'em. 'Jones is hiring you without those damn Referral Cards. And that could be the beginning of a real break-through!'

"James Flores scratches his head. 'But I thought that was supposed to be against the rules.'

"'Sure,' I shrug. 'But if the rules stand in the way of getting workers when the growers want 'em, they toss 'em out the window.'

"Just then, the trucks from Jones pull up outside and the workers start for the door. 'If the growers don't have to go by the rules, neither do we. From now on,' I tell 'em, walking out to the trucks, 'if anybody wants workers, they can damn well come down here to C.S.O. and pick 'em up. If they ask for those little pieces of paper, we'll have a roll of 'em right there on the desk.'

"As they leave, I kinda glide back into the office thinking no matter how many times it happens, it almost always comes as a big surprise. There's the enemy out there, Fred, and you keep fighting him all along the line. Then, while you're pushing hard at one particular spot, all at once you look around and find out you won a coupla victories someplace else, just because you never once let up on the pressure.

"But then, there's the other side of the coin, as you well know, Fred. Just let up on that pressure, even for a second, and see what happens. Like I saw!"

Everything had been going great at the Jones Ranch all week long. He was paying eighty-five cents an hour and taking on more workers every day. His trucks loaded up in front of the C.S.O. office every morning and unloaded there every night. It had all been just as smooth as clockwork. Cesar was just beginning to relax a little when the end of the week rolled around and the trucks rolled in, and the workers were "madder'n hell!"

"'We're gonna quit, Mr. Chavez!' one of 'em yells, as the women pile out of one truck and the men out of the other. All at once, I'm surrounded right there in the middle of the street in front of the C.S.O.

"'What's wrong?' I yell into the cackling crowd.

"'No more eighty-five cents an hour,' comes this woman's voice, louder than all the rest. 'Tomorrow, Jones pays by the crate.'

"'It's true, Chavez,' says Campos. 'The old speedup.' And then from all around me come the high, angry cries:

"'We're through!'

"'Send us to the flowers, Mr. Chavez!'

"I shoot both arms up, thinking, God, what a jerk to think it could last! When I finally get their attention, I ask 'em, 'You been doing OK on eighty-five cents an hour, haven't you?'

"'Sure,' yells Loudmouth, 'but tomorrow it's piece-work!' Then they all chime in again:

"'Jones double-crossed us!'

"'Lucky if we make three dollars a day!'

"'Now wait,' I quiet them, thinking, Christ! I can't let 'em quit! Gotta hold onto those jobs. 'You want the braceros to get your jobs?' Naturally they don't, but they aren't gonna tell me about it. They just look down, sorta mumbling.

"'OK, then.' I fold my arms. 'Soon as Jones tells you the rate tomorrow, turn it down. Just stand there and keep arguing with him.'

"'But, Mr. Chavez,' shouts Loudmouth, 'we can't keep arguing with him all day.'

"'I'll bet you could,' I kid her.

"'Na-a,' she kinda bleats, 'he'll just tell us we're through and bring in the braceros.'

"'Not if you stay right there,' I say, trying to jump over the talk and latch onto that idea I know is running around loose in my head somewhere. Then suddenly, up it pops—something I read in Saul Alinsky's book on John L. Lewis:

"'I tell you what,' I throw my finger out at them and snap it back. 'You stay right there, like I said. Don't even leave your row. Just sit down!'

"'Sit down?' says Loudmouth. 'And then?'

"'Then,' I tell 'em, 'if they bring in the braceros and try to kick us out, we'll have another labor dispute, just like last week. And Crittendon'll come and jerk the braceros out. Now then, how about it?'

"They just stand there, arms folded, shifting their feet, shooting their eyes at me and one another.

"'Come on.' I push 'em a little. 'Don't be afraid. All you have to do is stay there. We'll even slip in, after it starts, and be right with you. And while you're waiting, you'll be sitting.' I start laughing. 'Imagine that! Sitting down in the tomatoes! Brother, you never had it so good!'

"A couple of 'em start it, and then they're all rocking back and forth in the middle of the street, giggling.

"'OK?' I look around at them again. Most of 'em nod, still chuckling, looking down, making foot-drawings in the dirt. 'OK, see you in the morning, unh?' I start to ease out of the ring of workers to go into the office.

"As I open the door, one of 'em yells, 'No dejanos plantado con los tomates!' What it means is, 'Don't leave us planted out there with those tomatoes.' In other words, don't stand us up!

"As they're breaking up, I go in and phone James Flores to get ahold of

Angel, Chavira, Campos, Mejia and the union people for a meeting of the Employment Committee. We decide it would be a shame to keep our little 'sit-in' all to ourselves. So, while the rest of us are out there with the workers, James Flores will stay at the office and get the word to Crittendon and the State and Federal brass."

Chapter 13

The Sit Down

"The following morning, it happens! We're all sitting there, strung out along the tomato rows. It's ten a.m., an hour and a half since we slipped in with the workers after they fought with Jones and stopped work. I'm beginning to wonder what's happened to Crittendon when all at once here comes Zamora with a truckload of braceros. He puts 'em to work at the other end of the field and goes off toward the barn with Jones.

"Meantime, I'm wondering what in hell we're gonna do now. The 'locals' aren't just gonna sit there watching those guys clean up the field. If we don't do something, there's gonna be trouble. Somehow, I've gotta get to the braceros and see if we can keep 'em talking instead of working until Crittendon arrives. But if I go over there, Zamora's liable to see me and throw me out on my ass.

"I crawl down to Chavira and get him to slip over to the braceros. It works like a charm. Soon as they see him coming, they slack off. Just then Zamora comes out of the barn and spots 'em.

"'Hey, you guys!' he yells, running up to them. 'Get back to work!' Then they're all talking at once, the braceros real soft, Zamora loud. Finally, I hear him yell, 'All right, all of you shut up and listen to me! Anybody who isn't back on the job in two minutes goes out of here on the first bus for Mexico tomorrow!'"

Just then, someone passed by Cesar like a flash. It was Rachel! He tried to stop her, but she kept on going right up to where they were. Zamora threw her off the ranch, but she came over to where Cesar sat in the middle of the tomatoes and asked him for the keys to his car. Right in front of Zamora! Well, that fixed him up, too!

"As I'm leaving, I grab Angel. 'Now listen,' I tell him fast. 'It's all going our way. The braceros are with us; and even if they start working again, they aren't gonna hoe many tomatoes. Meantime, I'm gonna go get the bigshot from L.A. to come up here. Get the word to all the workers. Tell 'em to all sit tight 'til we get back.' I grab Rachel and Chavira and we take off.

"Back at my house in El Rio, I get on the phone and it sounds like things are moving. Crittendon left L.A. an hour before and oughta be arriving any second. James Flores tells me the State and Federal guys—even some 'observer' from Carr's office—are on their way, along with the local media.

"While I'm phoning, Fred, I can hear Chavira and Rachel arguing in the kitchen—something about picketing. When I finish, she comes in and reaches for the phone. I ask her, 'What's up?'

"'We're gonna picket!' she says. 'There's a strike out there. What good's a strike without pickets?'

"I tell her the workers are already picketing. Instead of walking, they're sitting down.

"'But we gotta show 'em we're behind 'em!' she says.

"I explained that they already knew that, Fred. And that all we had to do was get back out there with them until the brass showed up and there could be a showdown. If the workers lost, there would be plenty of time to talk about picketing. But if picketing started now, the workers would probably get all excited and pile into the braceros. Then the Sheriff would come out and throw all our guys in the clink.

"'So what! Then we'll have a real issue! Look, Cesar!' she says, starting to dial. 'You may be able to organize the Colonia, but don't tell me how to organize a strike!' She starts talking into the phone. 'Hello, Eddie? Look, I want you to line up some pickets right away—' She's still talking when Chavira and I get in the car and gun it for the ranch.

"'I don't think they'll get any pickets,' Chavira chuckles.

"'Why?'

"'Well, the workers all know that C.S.O. is doing what needs to be done. And the union, well, you know, Cesar,' he shrugs. 'It just wastes our time.'"

"We'd been at Jones' place only a couple of minutes when Crittendon's Chrysler whooshes up. As they start toward the workers, here comes Zamora.

"'Now look!'" Zamora shakes his finger in Crittendon's face. "'You got no right interfering in this. It's nothing but a wage beef between Jones and the workers.

"'I know my rights!' says Crittendon. 'Whatever I do is subject to review, of course. But I'm making the decisions here today.'

"'Well, by God!' Zamora swings away. 'I'm gonna call San Francisco and find out about this.'

"'That's your privilege,' Crittendon says quietly. 'Meantime, we're gonna try to work out a solution here.' He turns to me: 'Who's gonna represent the "locals"?' As the workers are taking a vote, James Flores and the State and Federal brass and a coupla reporters arrive.

"That's when the fun begins. The workers choose little Loudmouth, Chavira and Angel as their representatives. Loudmouth accuses Jones of going back on his word. Jones claims what he pays his workers is his own business.

"'Sure, it's your business,' Crittendon says. 'And if you can find some more "locals" who'll work by the crate, that's your business too. But with this valley loaded with unemployed "locals," if you put those Nationals to work, you're in trouble!' Then he turns to Cunningham (he's Hayes' buddy from San Francisco who made such a jackass out of himself at Juanita School. Remember, Fred?), 'What do you folks want to do about it?'

"Cunningham stands there shaking his head. 'Mr. Hayes—uh,' he catches himself just in time. 'The State wants no part of this mess.'

"'I guess not!' Zamora sneers.

"Crittendon swings around toward Jones and Zamora. 'Well, the *United* States does!' He booms it out. 'There's been a lot of monkey business going on around here, and it's gotta stop!' Then he settles down on Jones alone: 'So far, you've gotten off pretty damned easy, Mr. Jones. But just remember, you've got two violations chalked up against you. And if I file another complaint—'

"That does it, Fred. Not only does Jones give in but, with a little prod from us, he ups the ante to ninety cents an hour. Wow! Are those workers tickled! Hats in the air, coyote yells, and 'Viva's all over the place. They're out there, hard at it, in the tomatoes again about the time Rachel and Eddie come skidding up with the union picket signs!

"A few minutes later, while I'm talking to one of the reporters, damned if I don't notice some Japanese braceros! They're trimming and loading flowers for some guy who leases from Jones. I can tell the job won't last long, but every bit helps, you know. So I send James Flores back to the C.S.O. office for more 'locals' to replace the Japanese.

"That makes an even better ending to that story, Fred. Except, of course, it isn't the end. All it is is one less battle we have to win.

"The next one begins one afternoon about a week later when the trucks roll in from Jones Ranch. I can tell something bad has happened by the way they're all so quiet. Then, spotting me at the office door, one of 'em calls my name and that sets them all yelling:

"'They laid us off!'

"'More dirty tricks!'

"'They're up to something!'

"'That dirty rat Zamora!'

"When I finally get all the bits and pieces together, it's the same old story: Zamora showed up at Jones Ranch at quitting time and fired 'em all. No reason (so they say). Nothing. So with the workers all tight around me at the desk, I call Zamora.

"'Hear you laid 'em all off this afternoon,' I tell him.

"'That's right,' he says.

"'Why?'

"'That's my business.'

"'We'll see about that!' I bang him off and get through to Jones. His voice sounds kinda wobbly.

"'All I know, Chavez,' he says, 'Zamora claims they was water-grass mixed up with the seedlings in one of the loads, 'n', well, that costs me money, you know.'

"'So?' I wait, thinking, unh-hunh, so nobody did a thing! Water-grass just started sprouting outa the seedlings after they'd been picked!

"'Well, Christ! Chavez,' Jones sorta whines. 'I can't buck the Association, you know.'

"'No!' I'm almost yelling now. 'But you *can* buck the Federal Government and the C.S.O., can't you? OK, Jones,' I kinda sing it out. 'If that's the way you want it.' I slam the phone down and sit there wondering what else we can do to get those jobs back. So we can hold onto the workers.

"'Well,' yells a worker, 'whatcha gonna do now, Chavez?' I just look at her, thinking what I'd really like to do would be to get 'em all outa there so I can sit down with the Employment Committee and thrash this out more or less quietly. But if I do that, the workers'll figure we don't trust 'em.

"'We gotta have a meeting!' one of 'em yells. (Fred, you remember I told you before how when I first came to Oxnard the workers weren't used to meetings? They thought meetings were a waste of time? When stuff like this came up, they'd say, 'Oh, the hell with meetings! Let's go out there and throw those damned braceros outa the field!' But gradually, after I got 'em holding meetings and making plans, they thought it was great. Found out it was a wonderful way, I guess, to blow off steam. Better'n at home or even at a bar.)

"So now, when this Jones thing comes up, they gotta have a meeting. And what they'll do, they'll blow all that steam they're full of right out the window. Then tomorrow, when we really need it all to fight Jones and Zamora with, they'll all be like a bunch of empty flour-sacks. In a way, it's like by making a plan and a lotta noise, they fight tomorrow's battle now, right here in the office. So then what's the point of coming back here tomorrow for the real fight? No point at all. End of fight. End of jobs. End of any confidence they might have had in C.S.O. to help 'em win.

"Besides, Fred, this thing about the water-grass is something that should only be discussed with the Employment Committee. If you start discussing it with this mob and make just the tiniest hint that maybe somebody did throw a little grass in with those seedlings, whamo! you're against them! Against them? Hell, you're a grower, for God's sake!

"But anyway, Fred, sorta hoping they can be talked out of it, I ask 'em, 'Whataya want a meeting for?'

"'We gotta make a plan,' some guy yells.

"'Why?' I ask, coming up with the only plan I know. 'The plan is to go out there and demand those jobs, and see what Jones and Zamora do. Then we make our move. And so on, until we win. That's our plan.'

"But that's not good enough. See, Fred, it's just that you never like the plan you know about. What you want is some kinda secret scheme, something you never heard of. The excitement of the unknown, I guess.

"'Na-a, Chavez,' says some guy. (Check that, Fred, they're back to 'Chavez' again.) 'Tell us the real plan.'

"'Dios dirá,' I smile at 'em. 'God will say.' A few of them give me these sly looks that mean, 'Ah, Chavez has something up his sleeve, so we don't have to worry!'

"See, Fred, even if I did have a plan, I wouldn't tell 'em. You start laying that kinda stuff out to a whole mob of people more'n a minute or two before you go into action, you're dead. With a building or a street or something that just stays there, you can try Plan I and if that doesn't work you can go on to Plan II, etc. But if you start that way with a whole horde of people, you've got nothing but confusion. The only way to do it is to get 'em all on Plan I until just before you're ready to switch to Plan II. Then tell 'em and lead 'em in that direction. That's what's known as the O.T.A.T., Fred, the One Thing At a Time principle in mass organization!

"So I just sit there shaking my head. 'No,' I tell 'em. 'We've had these discussions before. The only thing we've got to find out are the ones that wanna go ahead and the ones that don't.'

"And it's right here, at times like these, that you find out how the people really feel about you. As long as you're right when you call the shots, nobody says anything. But the moment things get a little rough and you tell them they gotta carry part of the load, a few of 'em always get hot.

"'You know what I say?' some guy sings out. 'I say to hell with Jones!

Damned if I'm gonna kiss his ass for a lousy job!'

"This is one of those real brave-type guys, Fred. The kind the union always counts on heavy because they look like they're full of fight. Always the first ones to wanna strike because they don't really wanna work much to begin with. Then, when the going gets rough, they're the first ones to desert.

"I look at this guy hard. 'You like the gravy, but not the dirty work, uh?' Then I turn to the rest. 'Anyone else that doesn't wanna fight, now's the time to walk out.'

"'A-ah,' another guy says. 'You can't beat these growers. I don't care what Chavez says. They're too rich.'

"'No, Chavez,' someone else says. 'You weren't even born when we started this fight.'

"'You've got a lot to learn,' another guy pops off. I don't say anything. Some of them are just letting off steam. The others would just as soon have the whole thing flop just to prove they're right.

"'And if we fail?' asks someone. 'What happens then?'

"'Nothing happens,' I tell him.

"'But I got a family to feed,' comes this old, rough voice. And right here, Fred, is where it's awful easy to make a mistake, because the guy is trying to pull a double whammy on you. For one thing, he wants you to forget that the workers are human beings like everyone else and start treating them like they're something super-special. You gotta dress 'em and feed 'em and even wipe their behinds, for God's sake! But the second you do, you're dead; they make a horse's ass out of you from then on. In a way, it's tied in with being over-anxious to help 'em, like I already told you about before, Fred.

"The other thing this guy wants to remind you about is that you've got a good job, so you're gonna be OK regardless of what happens to him. He's right about this, too; but that's not the point. The point is that he's dragging it in to try and convince you to treat him like a 'poor little worker,' instead of like an ordinary human being. So the rug has gotta be jerked out from under him.

"I raise my hands from my lap and turn 'em over and tell him, 'Well, you didn't have a job before. So if we fail, you'll be the same way again. No job.'

"Soon as I say that, the muttering in there gets louder than ever. 'Sure, I know it's rough,' I tell 'em. 'But who were you complaining to before C.S.O. came to Oxnard? You didn't have a job then, either.'

"See, Fred, another thing you're up against in a thing like this is the old 'arena spirit.' You're the matador out there with the bull, and practically no one, not even your friends or the ones who agree with you, will come to your rescue. They just wanna see who's gonna win. It's entertainment.

"But thanks God! finally old Mejia speaks up: 'Señor Chavez is right. We've been through this many times. It's just up to us to get out there in the morning and go after 'em.'

"I look around hoping one of the women will speak. (Because, Fred, I found out that very often they're better'n men at times like this. It's not that they're really better; it's that, in one way, they're freer: they don't have the main burden for the family, so they don't have to be so cautious. But they also know they have to get the food on the table, whether the husband brings in the money or not. So they tend to be more militant. It seems like a contradiction, but I think it's true.)

"So anyway, while I'm trying to pick a few of 'em out with my eyes, all at once Carmen Ortega, this middle-aged woman on the Employment Committee, pushes to the front and faces them: 'We're all very tired,' she says in this sorta quiet voice. 'I think it would be a good thing for the ones that don't want to go ahead, let them stay out. But right now, the rest should all go home so we'll be rested for tomorrow.' Then she goes over and opens the door and stands there waiting for 'em to leave.

"That gets it. You could almost see some of those loudmouths shrivel up with shame. They can't even look her in the eyes as they go out the door. Pretty quick they've all gone except the Employment Committee members and Del Buono, Rachel, Eddie, and John."

Chapter 14

Poor Little Worker

———————

"Sitting down with them around the long table in the little room at the rear, I'm wondering how in hell I can get them to see the thing naked. You see, Fred, the more 'advanced' the workers are, the harder it is to get them to see workers as human beings with all the weaknesses human beings have. Now that some of 'em are 'developing,' they are beginning to be infected with the same 'poor little worker who can do no wrong' attitude that some of the rest of us who have been fighting for 'em have. That I have to be constantly on guard against in myself.

"Anyway, after they've kicked it around a little, I speak up: 'To be able to do a good job fighting 'em, we've gotta be able to understand exactly what their position is. So let's go back about ten or fifteen years, and—'

"'Ten or fifteen years!' Campos cuts in. 'But what about right now, Cesar? It's getting late.'

"'That's what I mean,' I tell him. 'I want to go back a ways because it is getting late. I wanna save time.'

"'Yeah,' gripes Mejia. 'But I can't go back that far. I've got five kids right now, today.'

"'I know,' I tell him, ignoring the 'poor little worker' deal he's pulling. 'But fifteen years ago there were no braceros in the United States, right?'

"'So what?' says Campos.

"'And we know they had plenty of seedlings then, right?'

"'I guess so,' says Campos. 'But come to think of it—'

"'Just pretend like it,' I tell him. 'So let's say we had a hundred workers out there cutting seedlings, and the grower found water-grass in the crates—'

"'So?' grunts Del Buono.

"'So,' I push it along, 'if the workers kept putting in the grass along with the seedlings and they got warned, and they still wouldn't quit, what do you think would have happened?' I look around the table, but nobody answers. 'Well, they woulda been fired, wouldn't they? Not because the grower wanted to replace them with braceros, but because he was losing money on his seedlings. So—'

"'But, Cesar,' Rachel catches me up, 'how can you believe there was grass in those seedlings?'

"'This is not a question of believing or not believing,' I tell her. 'This is what they're saying. And that's what we have to be able to beat, isn't it?'

"'But hell, Cesar!' Eddie says. 'You know they're just saying it as a pretext to get the "locals" out of the field, so they can bring in the braceros.'

"'Regardless,' I tell him, refusing to let 'em sidetrack me. 'They're still saying it! So, even though Jones is paying lousy wages and all, if he sells seedlings with grass in 'em, he'll lose money. Then the workers won't make any wages at all. They won't even be working!'

"'Oh, Cesar.' Del Buono gets this real fatherly look on his face. 'No es lo mismo ver morir, como cuando a uno le toca,' he quotes the old dicho meaning, 'It's not the same to see death as to die.' (More freely, 'It's easy for us who are not out there to judge the workers in the field!')

"Now I've got three of 'em playing to the grandstand, defending the 'poor little workers.' Of course, what they're saying, Fred, is about 99% true. But that's not the point. What I'm trying to get 'em to do is be honest and admit that there's a 1% chance that neither Jones nor Zamora is lying about that grass. If they'll do that and cut the crap about how we're all perfect and the other guy's a bastard, it'll be a real lesson for everyone. Not only for now, but for the future.

"But here again, Fred, we can't be honest with ourselves. The workers are afraid to point the finger at each other. As for the others, well, you can see for yourself how honest they're being! But I can't think of some kind of a painless way to bring it out until, all of a sudden, Del Buono, still pushing this fake defense of the workers, mentions that they're much too 'skilled' to mix grass with the seedlings. Right then it pings:

"OK,' I tell 'em. 'Let's take a journeyman carpenter, the most skilled guy in the trade. (My brother Richard is one, so I oughta know.) And say that guy hangs a lotta windows wrong. Now I don't care how many years' experience he's had, that carpenter's gonna get dumped, because the guy he's working for has got a responsibility to the ones he's selling those windows to. Right?'

"'Well, sure,' sneers Del Buono. 'But that's only one guy getting dumped—'

"'Right!' I practically pounce on him. 'You see the difference?'

"'Chavez is right.' Mejia sorta grins. 'Let's admit it, once in a while some worker gets a little careless and throws in some grass. I've done it myself. But why should all of us get canned because of one or two? That's the thing we gotta fight against.'

"'But how?' Chavira looks at me.

"'Come on, Chavira,' I tell him. 'You know the answer to that one. We just go out there and prove to him he's wrong and get those jobs back.'

"'Phooey,' Rachel sputters. 'We don't have to prove anything! By rights those jobs belong to our guys, and we'll either get 'em or throw a picket line around the place!'

"'OK, Rachel,' I nod. 'You just go right ahead and picket "by rights," and see if you get those jobs back.' I look at some of the workers. 'You folks know what happens when you pull a strike.' Nobody says a word, so I go on:

"'Lemme ask you something. What do you think would have happened to Pancho Villa with his two thousand Dorados against twenty thousand Federales, if he had drawn a line and said: "OK, this is where we draw the line, no more retreat?"'

"Mejia chuckles. 'He'd'a been slaughtered.'

"'So what did he do?' I ask 'em.

"'He waited and struck at night,' says Campos. 'Or in disguise. Or when he was pretty sure he could win.'

"'Oh, quit it, Cesar,' says Del Buono. 'That was a long time ago. And besides, it was in another country.' But he's too late. The comparison really pings into some of the old-timers. See, Fred, they're getting a kick because they know the rest didn't get it.

"'It's true,' says Campos. 'Most of us have been in strikes, and we know what happened.'

"'What did happen?' I ask.

"'We failed,' he shrugs.

"'Why?'

"'Well,' says the old man, 'they either brought in scabs to break our lines. Or we couldn't hold out as long as the growers. And then, if they couldn't beat us that way, they went to a judge and he threw us in jail, and the strike was broken.'

"'Yeah!' Eddie interrupts. 'But you weren't organized then.'

"'That's right,' I cut in. 'And would you say they're organized now? Oh, sure, I know the unions have tried in the past, and they told the workers if they picketed they'd win. But they didn't. So the workers found out the unions had lied to them. Pretty quick, there were no workers around anymore. Just the "union representatives." And that was the end of that.'

"Chavira chimes in. 'So are you telling us, Cesar, that if we picket, you pull out?'

"'No.' I kinda jerk my head away. 'What I'm saying is that we try the other first. That way, I think we'll get a few jobs and get rid of a few braceros. Also, that'll prove to the workers it can be done.'

"'But what if it doesn't work?' asks Rachel.

"I sorta brush the top of the table and tell her, 'We'll cross that bridge when we get there.

"Old man Campos pushes back from the table. 'I guess Cesar's right. We've gotta take some responsibility ourselves first. If it doesn't work, well—.' He puts on his hat and walks slowly out. The others follow him.

"When I finally hit the sack around two a.m., I just lie there thinking. I start to think how I shoulda let the workers picket and see who's right, me or the union. 'Course, if I were in their shoes, I'd probably wanna picket, too. Sure, I think, but not now while they're all broke. Wait'll they've got a few months' work under their belt and a few bill collectors off their back. But then I start asking myself what makes me think I know what's best for them when I'm not even a worker myself. But damnit! I think, I'm a helluva lot closer to being one of them than many of those damned loudmouths over there!

"Thinking of them, some of their faces start drifting by. Ruiz, for instance. I wonder if he'll stick. Jaramillo? No, better not count too much on him. What about—'

"And just then the alarm goes off. It's four a.m. I roll out and tear over to the office.

"When I get there, damned if five or six of the workers aren't already there under the overhang. Now wouldn't you think, Fred, when a guy stays up all night preparing for something, he oughta at least be allowed to be the first one on hand in the morning to get it going? Oh, well, that's life for you!

"Inside the office, things start off pretty much as usual. While I'm phoning John and James and some of the others to get their behinds outa the sack, the workers are sweeping up and putting on the coffee. Then I turn into a 'worker-watcher' keeping my eye on the door, checking out front and behind for workers. There's not a one in sight!

"Back inside, the first kernel comes popping out of my head, and I phone Villanueva, C.S.O. Vice President, who's got this early-morning, Spanish-language radio program. Along with a 'beeper' with a telephonic hookup.

"'Good morning, Cesar,' he says, and it's going right over the air while we're talking. All the stuff that happened out at Jones' place yesterday. (And that's Plan I, Fred!)

"'Tell me, Cesar,' he says, 'what's going on down at the C.S.O. office this bright and ice-cold Southern California morning?'

"'Oh, hay menudo,' I tell him. 'A lot of little things.' Soon as I say that word 'menudo,' another little kernel pops because, as you know, Fred, menudo is also a very delicious dish that Mexican people love to have in the morning, especially after a rough night. So I tell Villanueva:

"'Oh, and by the way, Mr. C.S.O. Vice President, we've got a little surprise down here for the workers this morning—menudo!' (And that's Plan II, Fred!)

"'Menudo!' he says, like he can hardly believe it. 'Gee, those workers are sure lucky. Well, Cesar, what's up for today?' I tell him that all depends on Jones and Zamora, and right away he puts on this record, 'Tu ya no Soplas,' which is all about this bastard who goes around double-crossing everybody. Of course, he dedicates it to our friends Zamora and Jones!

"Pretty quick, the first worker calls in: 'Is it true about the menudo?' he wantsa know.

"'Why, certainly,' I tell him. 'Compliments of Zamora.'

"'How come?' he asks me.

"'Oh, he's worried about your health,' I tell him. 'He wants to be sure you're good and strong so you can get those jobs back out there.' After a coupla more calls, it's pretty clear they're biting; so I send over to Maria's Restaurant for a big pot of menudo. Before long, a lot of the workers are there at the office eating and joking, offering to give donations for their breakfast.

"'No,' I tell 'em. 'I'm gonna get double from you later on. When you get your first check from Jones.'

"'Aw!' One of 'em flips his fingers up. 'We just came down for the eats. We're not gonna work.'

"'Oh, well,' I kinda smile and shrug, 'then I'll lose, I guess.'

"By now, it's around six-thirty a.m., and still no trucks from Jones. So (Plan III), I get old man Garcia to start telling everyone that's got a car to go home and get it. Then (Plan IV), I grab Carmen Ortega, Chavira, and old man Campos!

"'You better go out there right now,' I say to them. 'Tell Jones you wanna go to work. He'll probably say there is no work. But don't argue with him or trample his tomatoes. Just wait.'

"'But what will we do, Mr. Chavez?' says Carmen. 'We can't just—'

"'Yes, you can,' I cut in. 'You just stay there, right by the little office in the barn. If he tells you to leave or threatens to call the cops or anything, you just tell him C.S.O. phoned the United States Department of Labor guy. This guy said for the workers to wait because he's on his way up here to settle this thing, OK?'

"They're just leaving when James Flores and his brother, Eddie, and Rivera, my best Service Center helper, show up; and we start organizing the rest of the operation (Plan V). Eddie will hold down the office and phone Carr and Crittendon about what's happened. James will be my 'runner' at the ranch. I'm wondering what the hell I'll do with Rivera when, all at once, I get this spy idea (Plan VI) and deploy him out on the highway with the idea of tailing all State and Federal cars.

"By the time James and I get to the ranch, the braceros are already working and the 'locals' are scattered all along the edge of the field. James is just starting to pull 'em all together when Jones comes out of his office by the barn.

"'Hey, Chavez!' he yells. 'You better get those people out of here or I'm gonna have to call the Sheriff!'

"So I say, 'Well, only reason we're here, we wanna work. All we're doing, we're just waiting for the Federal guys.' Then I get thinking of something I heard Crittendon tell Jones before. 'You know,' I tell him, it'll be a lot easier on you, Mr. Jones, if we get this problem solved.'

"'I have no problem,' he says. 'Who says I have a problem?'

"'They all think you have.' I jerk my head toward the workers. 'You know, we already got Crittendon up here twice, Mr. Jones. If he has to come up here a third time, you know what's probably gonna happen to your braceros.'

"Well, Fred, you know how it usually goes in a situation like this. First, the people are all scattered. Then the argument begins and they all start bunching up. The longer it goes on, the tighter they get around you. That's how it is right now, me telling Jones how we're gonna keep after those jobs 'til we get 'em, Jones kicking the ground with his boot, and the workers pressing in.

"Then, all at once, Jones jerks his head up like he just had an idea and his hand shoots out at me. Right at the same time I heard this kind of a low crowd-moan, and old Rough-voice, clear at the back, yells, 'Hey, don't do that, you son of a bitch!'

"'But I just want to tell you something.' Jones stands there with his hands out now, and this look in his eyes like he's kind of pleading. And oh, my God, Fred, I feel so lousy! This is the last thing I wanted to happen.

"'I'm sorry,' I shake my head. Then turning to the workers, I tell 'em, 'No, no, don't say things like that.' I kinda feel like they're my own kids.

"'Por qué?' Rough-voice yells. 'Why not?'

"'Véngase!' I motion to him. 'Come up here.'

"He comes up, big and tough and very mad. 'You have no right to tell me that, Chavez!' He stands there breathing hard, his huge chest puffing out and those big arms hanging sort of out from his body. But you know, Fred, he doesn't scare me. I guess I'm so worried about a big riot or something, I forget to be scared of getting socked myself. So I just look up at him:

"'No tiene motivo para este.' I keep on shaking my head a little. 'He's not giving you any reason to do this.'

"The big worker holds out his arms with those two big fists on the end, looking from me to Jones. 'No,' I tell him, holding up both hands and thinking, Christ! I just can't stand here saying 'no' all day. Then this real corny thing hits me: 'Acuérdate, Señor, hay mujeres aquí, y senoritas.' I stretch my arms out toward the crowd. 'Remember, there are women here, and young girls.' Zingo, it's like magic! The big guy starts back, you know, and turns around toward the people:

"'Excuse me, ladies.' He even kinda bows his head a little bit. Then he turns and pats me on the shoulder, shakes hands with Jones, and goes back into the crowd. (And that was Plan VII!)

"'Now what were you gonna say, Mr. Jones?' I ask him.

"'Well,' he kicks his boot again. 'I been giving you guys a lotta work lately. How come you're always picking on me?'

"'No, that's not it, Mr. Jones,' I tell him. 'All we want, we just want you to play square with us. That's all. But you go ahead and lay off a whole crew of workers with families to support, just because one or two of the guys throw grass in the crates. You think that's being fair, Mr. Jones?'

"'Maybe you're right, Chavez,' he says, looking around at the people. 'I know a lot of you folks have big families and all. So if you'll give me an honest day's work, I'll hire you.'

"I kinda strain forward, I guess: 'Can they go to work now?'

"'Sure,' he nods. Then he straightens up and looks around at the crowd: 'But C.S.O. or no C.S.O., the first one I catch throwing grass is gonna get fired!' I repeat in Spanish what he said, and they all start smiling and clapping in a real friendly way.

"'Jones' face lights up. 'What are we waiting for?' he shouts, throwing his arms up in the air.

"'A trabajar!' I yell. 'Let's go to work!'

"Well, Fred, they've hardly picked up their hoes when here comes that big black Cad over the irrigation ditch, and Zamora jumps out and stops them. 'What's going on here?' He looks at Jones.

"Jones starts to burn a little bit: 'Well, I just hired the "locals,"' he says.

"'What in hell for?' yells Zamora.

"Jones is looking down, tapping his boot: 'Well, they all came out, and—'

"'Wait a minute!' Zamora takes him aside. James, Chavira, and I go right along. 'What do you guys want?' asks Zamora.

"'Oh,' I kinda grin. 'I guess we just want to be part of the conversation.' Zamora grunts, grabs Jones' arm, and they both go into the office by the barn.

"I can't hear 'em, but I can see the whole thing going on. First, Jones puts his arms out like he's pleading. Then Zamora starts pounding the table. Finally, Jones just stands there scratching his head.

"'I'll bet Zamora wins,' says James. And sure enough, about a second later, damned if Jones doesn't start nodding. Next thing, here he comes tearing out of the office to where our guys are working. I send Chavira out to tell them to stay right where they are. Actually, it isn't even necessary: the workers are already sitting down along the rows that they've been working!

"Pretty quick, here's Jones again in his pickup. He comes up toward us slow but still not completely stopping. I tear over to him, yelling, 'Are you leaving, Mr. Jones?' He nods. 'But what about the workers?' I've got my hand on the car door, walking along with him.

"'You'll have to ask Zamora,' he says, moving real slow as several of us surround the truck. Finally, he stops and looks at us, shaking his head. 'I don't know,' he says. 'I just don't know. Between the C.S.O. and the State people and the Federal people and Tafoya (his chief competitor) and this'—he pulls a piece of water-grass out of his pocket—'you guys are gonna ruin me.'

"I stick my head inside the cab: 'Mr. Jones,' I say, 'you know who's gonna ruin you? Zamora, and the big growers who tell you what to do.'

"'No, Chavez.' He looks down at the dashboard. 'This is a labor matter. He's my representative.'

"Just then here comes your friend, Fred, 'Pretty Boy' Morales. (It turns out he is Crittendon's flunkie in Santa Barbara.) We beat Zamora over to him, and I let him have it:

"'OK, Morales,' I tell him. 'You know what's going on here. What are you gonna do about it?'

"'Oh, I can't get involved in this, Mr. Chavez.' He raises his hand like he's pushing himself away from us. 'I'm just here as an impartial observer.

"'Impartial observer, hell!' I rip into him. 'You're getting paid to do a job. If you're afraid of your friend Zamora here, why don't you let someone else take over?'

"'Mr. Chavez,' he says with one of these phony, crumbly smiles, 'you're impossible. You guys accuse me of being pro-grower, and Zamora here'—he winks at the Assocation boss—'he accuses me of being pro-worker. So I'm just caught in the middle.' With that, he goes over and starts chatting with Zamora, just to prove how impartial he is!

"Right then, Plan VIII pops out of my little popper. I tell it to James Flores and he phones his brother at the C.S.O. office and learns that Crittendon is definitely on his way. Then we go up to Morales again:

"'Look, Morales,' I tell him, 'time's a-wasting. There's a labor dispute here. You better pull those braceros out 'til it's settled.'

'Oh, I can't do that, Mr. Chavez,' he says, batting his eyelids at Zamora sorta nervously. 'I'm just here to get the facts for our San Francisco people. It's up to them to make the decision.'

"'Hell!' I tell him. 'By the time you get a decision from those guys it'll be next week. The "locals" can't just sit out there all that time.' Morales just shrugs. So I pull this little reverse twist under Plan IX.

"'OK then,' I tell him. 'If you won't pull out the braceros, then you better get the "locals" outa here. Otherwise, there's liable to be trouble.'

"'No,' Morales says. 'I'm completely neutral on this thing.'

"'Well, by God, I'm not!' says Zamora, starting toward the workers.

"I stop him: 'They won't mind you, Zamora,' I tell him. 'They might even beat you up, after the way you been treating 'em. No, it's gotta be someone "impartial," like Morales here.' See, Fred, I figure if I can get Morales to do it, it'll really get him in Crittendon's doghouse. Also, it'll get Crittendon even more on our side. Besides, it's sorta like reverse 'divide and conquer'! And the way Morales has been sucking up to Zamora and the big growers, he's got it coming.

"'No,' says Morales, his eyes blinking real fast and sorta crazy. 'I think we better wait for Crittendon.'

"'Is he coming?' I try to act real surprised. You see, Fred, I figure if we can make Morales think that Crittendon is not coming, then with Zamora after him like he is to get rid of the "locals," Morales will think he's just got to make that decision.

"'Well, didn't you call him?' Morales' eyes are batting harder than ever now.

"'No,' I tell him, real innocent. 'You think we should?'

"At that, Morales gives Zamora this real wilty look and walks out to where the workers are with all the rest of us in tow. He tells them about how he's waiting for a decision from his superiors and, meantime, they probably better all leave the fields and go home.

"It couldn'ta been timed any better. Just as the workers are moving toward the barn, with us coming up in the rear, who should come zooming up but Crittendon and a guy from Secretary of Labor Mitchel's office named Flannery—along with Bates and Turner. Soon as I spot 'em, I whisper to James it would probably be a good idea if he let Crittendon know what his boy Morales had just done.

"'Even better, Cesar,' he says, 'why not get one of the workers to tell him?' So in a coupla minutes, right while Crittendon is talking to Jones, here comes Carmen Ortega pushing up to the front:

"'I want to talk to Mr. Crittendon,' she says.

"'Yes?' He looks at her real fast, almost like he's surprised as hell a worker can really talk or something, Fred.

"'I'm Carmen Ortega, and I want to ask you something,' says Carmen. 'When we came out here, Mr. Jones was very happy to have us start working and all. Right, Mr. Jones?' She turns and looks up at him. But he just kind of looks away. 'Well, anyway, he did, Mr. Crittendon. Then Mr. Morales comes out there and makes us stop. Now what I want to know, if you people are here to help us, how come Mr. Morales tells us to stop when Mr. Jones tells us to go?' (And there, Fred, on the point of that blade, came Plan X.)

"'Mr. Crit—Mr. Crittendon,' Morales kinda squeals, this real frantic look on his face, 'I think I can clear this up—'

"Crittendon puts up his hand, shutting Morales off. 'Let her talk!' he barks. 'Now then, let me get this straight, Miss Ortega—'

"'That's right!' Rachel butts in. 'Everybody knows Morales is the boss's man!'

"'Now wait a minute, Miss Jurado!' Crittendon mispronounces her last name. (It's really Guajardo, you know.) 'I can't be dealing with both the C.S.O. and the union!'

"'Why not?' Rachel says.

"'Because C.S.O. tells me one thing and you folks tell me something else.'

"Well, yeah, but—'

"'Please, Miss Jurado?' He keeps mispronouncing her name.

"'We have the workers themselves, right here,' I tell him. 'They have elected Mrs. Ortega, Mr. Campos, and Mr. Chavira to represent them. I think they should be the ones to speak.'

"Just as they had begun to tell Crittendon and Secretary Mitchel's man the score, I hear old man Campos' voice: 'You know, while we're here arguing, those braceros are out there working.'"

"'Where?' asks Crittendon.

"'Right out there behind that windbreak,' says James. With that, the workers all start yelling, pointing their fingers at the braceros.

"'Morales,' Crittendon yells, 'I want you to go out and pull those Nationals out of there, right now!' Morales slinks off toward the braceros, and Jones just sorta wilts down into his boots as he tells the 'locals' they can go back to work right after lunch.

"At that, Fred, the workers break up into little groups under the eucalyptus trees along the edge of the field and start to prepare their meal. Some of 'em are gathering wood, some build fires, and the rest start warming tortillas over the coals, spooning in the frijoles, and dousing the whole thing with chile picante. M-m, delicious, Fred.

"The rest of us are about to take off for lunch, when our 'spy,' Rivera, tears up and accuses Morales and Turner and Bates of playing 'footsie' with the growers. Early that morning, he had tailed them out to the Association, where they had yakked with Zamora for a while before coming out to Jones' place. Crittendon doesn't say a word. He just shoots Morales this filthy look and offers to treat us to lunch at the Blue Onion.

"As we are leaving, the 'locals' start getting up from under the trees and I watch 'em go back to work. Most of 'em are women, you know, and they've got these Levis on that come tight on their legs clear down to their Army shoes. Above the pants are the men's shirts with the long tails hanging down outside so they can bend easy, and so you can't see their behind every time they lean over.

"Then they have these scarves, Fred, all different colors. They wear them on their head and bring 'em down around their cheeks and over their nose to help protect them against pesticides, so all you can see is their eyes and the top of their nose.

"Then they have these hats with the brim about ten feet wide. When they're out there in the field with the sun in back of 'em, throwing a shadow out, what it is, Fred, it's like a lot of great big hats moving down the rows with nobody under 'em.

"When we go into the Blue Onion, I spot Vuovitch and Hartford and the rest of the grower-brass sitting at one of those mile-long booths. And you know, Fred, as soon as the Government guys see 'em—it's sort of an automatic thing—instead of going to a booth with us, they make a beeline for the growers. Just like a bunch of little lambs!

"We take a booth directly across from them, on the other side of this low partition, John and James and Rachel and Eddie and me. After a little while, I get up and go over to the other booth and look at the Government guys:

"'Well,' I kinda smile at them. 'I guess what we been saying about you guys is right.'

"Crittendon looks up and says, 'What are you talking about, Cesar?'

"I give this quick shrug: 'We walk into the place together and you guys head straight for the growers. What about us over there? Can't we at least have one of your minor officials sit with us and keep us company?'

"'Oh, oh,' says Crittendon. 'I just came over here because, uh—well, I'll go over there.'

"'No, don't bother,' I tell him. 'I just thought I'd make my point. Now that the situation has come up.'

"'I'll be right over,' he says, squeezing out of the booth.

"'No, it's all right,' I tell him. 'You don't have to if you don't want to. I just thought I'd remind you again, that's all.' With that, I go back to our booth, with Crittendon right behind me.

"Afterwards, we take him and the guy from Mitchel's office and Bates and Turner to the C.S.O. office, show 'em the latest complaints, and kid with them for a while. This is the first time any of 'em, except Crittendon, had ever been to the C.S.O. When they're investigating a complaint, they just go to the Association, never to us. The only places we ever meet with 'em are at the 'trouble spots'—like this morning at Jones' place—or on the boulevard, or the street corner, or wherever we happen to bump into 'em, you know.

"Anyway, while we're kidding away there, I let 'em know that I'm sure they think we're just a bunch of little brown animals. But that after they've been around us a little more, they'll find out we're just as human as the growers. Maybe more so. I tell 'em I realize that even though they probably feel more comfortable with the growers, they shouldn't get the idea they'll have to let us take a leak on their shoes before we'll be willing to talk to them!

"What it is, I s'pose, Fred, they're afraid the growers will find out they've been talking to us. But whatever the reason, I'm not kidding you, this is the very first time they ever came to our office. I guess you could call it some kind of a humiliating-type victory.

"Anyway, by the time they leave I get thinking, from the way we're getting a little closer to each other and the way things worked out this morning, that maybe, finally, we're getting somewhere in this unemploy-ment fight. In fact, I'm so sure of it that I'm just picking up the phone to break the news to Tony Rios at the national C.S.O. when, a good two hours before they're due, the trucks roll in from Jones Ranch."

Chapter 15

Slinging Bull

"I can tell there's something wrong. It isn't just that they're quiet, like before. It's the way they get off the truck, you know, not kidding or joking or taking their sweet time about it, but sort of in a hurry. Because generally, when they come in from work, they start hollering, 'Hey! What's up!' you know. 'What's going on?' 'What's cooking?' you know. Things like that, Fred. When they get off the trucks and come in the office, they just take it easy. They're tired. They even walk tired.

"When there's trouble, like now, they don't walk tired. They come walking so fast, it's sorta like a stampede right up to where I'm standing there at the door:

"'What happened?' I holler.

"'Zamora fired us again!' the guy at the head of the line yells. For a second, I'm really surprised. But almost instantly I'm disgusted as hell with myself for letting my guard down that way.

"'Why?' I kinda squeal.

"'He put the braceros back in and claims we can't keep up with 'em.'

"Then they all pour past me into the office.

"As we start the discussion, immediately they're all accusing me. They don't say it in so many words, but from the tone of their voices and the way they put things, they're trying to make me responsible for what had happened.

"Even though I know it's natural, Fred, I resent it; and finally I get fed up: 'OK,' I tell 'em. 'If that's the way you people feel, then there's no use trying to do anything. If you don't want the jobs, then we just won't fight. But remember,' I raise my voice a little, 'it'll take you twenty years and you still won't have a job unless you stick it out *now*. Clear to the end. Until everything's decided.'

"One of 'em yells, 'So what are you gonna do about it?'

"'I'm not gonna do anything,' I tell him. 'But what we can do, the only thing we can do, is exactly what we did this morning: go out there and battle for those jobs again.'

"'Well, yeah,' one of the women pops off, 'but how long can you keep that up?'

"'Long as you wanna job,' I tell her. 'Or until you break the grower down, and he knows you're gonna keep on doing it every time he tries to push you around.' Then I kinda look around the room at 'em: 'You know why they're hiring and firing you every day like they're doing?

"'Trying to break us down,' Campos says.

"'That's right!' I jump on it. 'Until you have a hundred workers out there today, tomorrow seventy-five, next day fifty, pretty soon one, and then none. This is how they figure they're gonna beat you. Unless you make up your minds you want those jobs and you're gonna go out and fight for 'em!'

"'We got paid today,' one of 'em says. 'So we really don't have to work tomorrow. 'Course, it would be nice to get those jobs.'

"'Look,' I tell 'em, 'if you wait one or two days—' But that's when I run out of gas. I'm not sure how to put it. And yet I'm really desperate, Fred, to do it just right. Or it won't sink in.

"I start over again: 'See, the only way you can hold onto those jobs is by not admitting you ever lost 'em. You must not admit it to Jones or Zamora or anyone. Not even to yourselves.' (Here, Fred, I'm thinking about the way the 'Little-guy-with-the-bottle,' Enclan, worked it.)

"'See,' I tell 'em, 'if you let one or two days go by, and then you go out there, that's like admitting that you were fired. That you're just a bunch of brand-new workers trying to get hired. And that'll be a longer, harder fight. But if we go out there tomorrow as though nothing had happened and claim our jobs, that's not admitting anything. And it'll probably be a lot easier to get 'em back.

"Well, but you know how they are, Fred. When some guy gets fired and you tell him sure he got fired all right but he's gotta go ahead and act like he didn't, it's pretty hard for him to understand it. He got fired and he knows he got fired; and that's it, period. End of argument.

"Times like this, what they really want, Fred, they want you to pull some kind of a super-miracle out of your hat and hand it to 'em. When you don't, a few get restless and start leaving. But most of 'em don't give up yet; they figure somehow we can get the jobs and beat the growers right there at the office. All we have to do is have a meeting!

"'Well,' I tell 'em, 'we're having a meeting.' When I say that, the grumbling gets even louder than before. With the workers, you can't get away with that stuff, you know. What they want, of course, they want you to call a real formal-type meeting, with the President of C.S.O. presiding.

"So I call Del Buono over at his nursery, and he hurries down and starts this sort of a 'near-meeting.' I didn't have time to tell him what had gone on, so I have to keep feeding him little bits of stuff all the way along. And you know what happens at a meeting, Fred, when you're repeating a lot of stuff the people know already and didn't want to hear about in the first place. They get bored and restless. Pretty quick, they aren't there!

"That's what happens here! They start leaving. There's no decision whether they're gonna come back or they're not gonna come back. Nothing. It's just sort of 'Well, we don't know.' (Personally, Fred, I don't think they are. I coulda bet my last penny on it.) So what happens, things are just left up in the air. They don't even adjourn the meeting. The people just walk out, you know. Disgusted.

"Only a little handful stay: old man Campos, Chavira, Carmen Ortega, Mary Jimenez, and a few more. These are the ones that have sort of played a part already. The workers picked them out there at Jones' place to represent them, and they spoke up. So now they're trapped, they can't walk out.

"This is what those guys want,' says Campos. 'Those growers are gonna keep on doing this for the next five years.'

"'That's right,' I tell 'em. 'We're gonna have this over and over unless we keep the pressure on. One or the other of us is gonna have to give in.' For a second I look around at them. 'I'm sure it's gonna be the grower, when he sees it's not gonna be us.'

"Soon as I say it, Mary Jimenez's kid brother jumps up: 'You know what?' he says. 'Count me in. I'll be there tomorrow morning!' The rest of 'em smile and sorta wink at me.

"'That's all I need,' I say, looking at the young kid. 'Just one. I'll go with you!'

"Well, Fred, on that happy note as they say, we phone Crittendon's office, leave a message about what's happened at Jones Ranch and go home to eat.

"An hour later, we're back at the office helping with all the other work that has to be done. The Employment Fight is the main thing, of course, Fred, but every night there's a steady trickle of people bringing in their problems. A lot of 'em are too rough for Rivera and the volunteers to handle without my help.

"So here you are with all the worry and pressure from the Employment Fight and, on top of that, you've got to keep helping these people that are coming in to the office one at a time. It's such a big letdown from being with the crowd of workers a while ago that, once in a while, as you sit there working away on the individual cases, you feel like you've hit bottom. It seems so kinda mild, Fred, as compared with the employment thing. And yet at one time these personal services kept many of us from getting a good night's sleep.

"Anyway, along about eleven p.m., with only the 'hard little handful' of us still there in the office, Crittendon calls to say he's here in Oxnard to help us out in the morning. We're happy as hell, but the big problem is still there: getting the workers. You see, Fred, if we can't get all of 'em, it'll look bad. We've got to get all the ones we had and maybe a few more to show we're growing, you know.

"But still, you can't go out there to the workers and kiss their butts to come back, either. (I already told you what would happen then.) You just gotta get 'em without letting 'em know you're after 'em. But how? I'm still beating my brains when the first phone call comes through. It's one of the workers, Ruiz, the one that phoned this morning about the menudo.

"'Well,' he says, 'what have you done?' He's had something to eat and gotten a little rested, so he's not quite as discouraged as he was before.

"'Not a thing,' I tell him. 'What have you done?'

"'Wha—uh, well,' he kinda stutters. 'I thought by now you'd have some plans—'

"'No,' I cut in. 'I'm not gonna do anything. Not until tomorrow morning, anyway, when you guys come back—if you come back—and we go out there to Jones Ranch again and have it out with them. That's all I know to do. Got any ideas?'

"'Well, no,' Ruiz says. 'But to tell the truth, I don't think we're getting anyplace at all. In three days it's been the same old thing. How long do you think it'll be before we can go out there and really go to work?'

"I can tell he's a little worried, so I really let it go on him: 'Well, it may be five years or it may be five days or it may be only five minutes from the time we get out there in the morning. Who knows?'

"'Que será, será.' He gives me a kind of a dirty chuckle. 'What's to be will be, uh, Chavez? Well, I knew that before I called you up.' He goes on giving me the needle. And right while he's talking, Fred, Plan XI suddenly falls into place:

"'Look, Mr. Ruiz,' I cut in. 'Here's something I'll bet you didn't know. There's this committee going around right now to talk to some of the workers that've been phoning to tell us they want to go out to Jones' place tomorrow. And also,' I keep spreading it on, 'there's a whole mountain of people coming into the office here to let us know they're with us.

"'In fact'—this time I go all out— 'I think that out of all those hundred people working at Jones Ranch, only about five or ten haven't come back.'

"'Oh, yeah?' he says, all excited. 'OK, Chavez, I'll see you.' He hangs up real fast. The 'old faithfuls' and I are still laughing over all that bull I was slinging when the phone rings again:

"'You know,' says this guy, 'I just seen old Ruiz at the store getting his lunch and stuff to take to work tomorrow. He says a lotta people are going back to Jones'. Is that true?'

"'It sure is,' I tell him.

"'Well, how come I didn't know about it?' he wantsa know.

"'You haven't been to the office,' I tell him.

"'A lot of people?' he asks.

"'Most of 'em,' I tell him. 'Come to think of it, I guess you're about the only one that hasn't been in.'

"'Is that right,' he says.

"'Sure,' I pile it on. 'They're all going back tomorrow. We're meeting here at four a.m. to discuss some pretty important stuff.'

"'Like what?' he wantsa know.

"'Only the ones that come in to make a fight for it will know when they come in the morning. If you wanna know, come on in.'

"'I know what it is,' he says. 'We'll go out there and we'll argue and we'll get another day's work. Then they'll run us off again.'

"'Excuse me,' I tell him. 'But there's a lotta people around here and we gotta start getting prepared for tomorrow. I'll see you, uh?' I ring him off and look around at the almost empty office!

"Then a whole flock of 'em start calling in. I keep yelling (at practically nobody) to 'Quiet down! I can't hear!' so the guy on the line will think there's a big mob in there, you know. And also because I want the 'old faithfuls' to listen to me telling the guys on the line about how everybody's coming back. That way, they'll start kinda half-believing it themselves. Even if it is a big lie so far, you know.

"Well, Fred, I always knew lies travel fast, but this time it's like lightning! The way it works, first a few of the workers just drift by outside and sorta peek in as they pass. Then, little by little, they start coming in, until there's around twenty-five in there with us. By now I've upped the ante to where I'm telling the ones who call in that the way things are going, we're gonna have the biggest crew in history at Jones Ranch in the morning!

"After a while, they all drift out again, the phone quits ringing, and only the 'old faithfuls' and I are left in the office. Of course, things look a lot better than they did, but I'm still worried. I kinda think they'll come back. But I'm just one, sorta by myself.

"'You think they'll come back?' I ask 'em.

"'Well, chee!' Mary Jimenez says, 'I don't know. It's possible. But I really don't know.'

"'Oh, sure,' Chavira chimes in, sorta believing my propaganda. 'We'll have a real mountain of 'em out there tomorrow. We'll have an even better show than yesterday.'

"I look over at old man Campos. 'Well, they may come back,' he says. 'Eighty-five cents an hour's better'n they can make in the carrots. And they can't get any decent work anywhere else. The only thing is, the other times they let 'em go they didn't get paid off. But this time they did. This is the worst thing. They may want to go back, you know, but this of being paid off makes the layoff complete. There's no reason to go back. Like there woulda been if they still had to pick up their pay.'

"'He's right, too, Fred. They've never done this before. Like Alinsky says, 'It's outside their experience.'

"By the time I get home it's one a.m., and I go to bed with my boots on. Next thing I know, there's this loud burr-r-r-r. I'm back in my old job at the lumberyard in San Jose, and the quitting signal's buzzing. Burrr-r-r-r! it goes again. Now it's the buzzer to start work in the morning; I pull the switch and send the first boards down the chain.

"But the damn thing won't stop. It's starting to bother the hell outa me when, all at once, I hear Helen's voice: 'Hey, Cesar,' she nudges me. 'It's four o'clock. Turn off the alarm.'

"'Yeah?' I shove in the electric buzzer and look at the clock. Hell! it's five after four. I guess those five minutes got lost, Fred, among the boards I was heaving onto that chain.

"I grab my coat and get outa there. All the way to the office I'm praying they'll show up. When I get there, I sit for a minute rubbing the sleep outa my eyes. When I look up, thanks God! I spot some of the same old early birds crouching together in the doorway outa the cold.

"Inside, it's just like the day before all over again. Some of the workers clean up, we serve coffee and pan dulce, and I get on the radio again with Villanueva. In fact, with everything the same as it was, almost exactly, and me with hardly any sleep for the last three days, pretty quick I get thinking it is yesterday. And I can tell what's gonna happen next, like a movie you've seen before. What's the word, Fred? Oh, yeah, 'déjà vu.'

"Anyway, just then James Flores comes in and sits down beside me: 'Well, what do you think?' I ask him.

"'I think there's gonna be trouble,' he says. 'Probably worse than yesterday.'

"'I think so, too.'

"'Ya got any ideas?' he asks me.

"'I haven't got anything,' I tell him. But even while I'm saying it, all at once my old neons snap on and here comes the beginning of Plan XII. 'Except for one thing,' I tell him. 'It's about time we got a lot of other people worried about this thing. And I mean a lot!'

"'How about the radio?' James asks me.

"'Too much money,' I tell him. 'We gotta do something that'll spread this thing.'

"'Yeah,' he says. 'All over Oxnard.'

"'All over the whole state!' I almost yell. 'Crittendon's OK, but if we don't get Carr's office and the government guy from San Francisco down here pretty damn quick, our friend Crittendon's liable to cave in with all the pressure!'

"'How we gonna do it?' James wantsa know.

"'Gotta think of something.' I kinda squeeze my head with both hands. It feels like a logjam inside there.

"By now it's six-thirty a.m., and the workers start coming fast. As they come, we load them into cars and taxi them out to the ranch and through the gate and up to the barn. Jones doesn't say a word. Just watches us dump our loads and go back to get some more.

"By the time we get them all out there, here comes Crittendon. He doesn't even stop. Just sort of dips his head as he drives by and takes the service road out to where the braceros are working, and pulls 'em out!

"And what it really is then, Fred, is an absolute replay of what happened yesterday. Jones is moaning and pleading, Crittendon is bawling the hell out of him and putting the 'locals' to work and taking off for L.A.; James is tearing back to the office and I'm taking off for some coffee at my place in El Rio.

"About twenty minutes later, I'm heading for the office feeling fine because I'm just about one hundred percent positive nothing's going to go wrong at the ranch this time. I'm just passing the F.P. trailer they put in about a week ago (at our request) when, all at once, something catches my eye. It's old eye-batting Morales' station wagon and a bunch of the Jones Ranch 'locals' piling out of it.

"'Hey, you guys!' I yell at 'em. 'What do you think you're doing?'

"'Getting Referral Cards,' one of 'em yells back.

"I jump out of the car and start shouting even before I come up to where they are: 'What happened this time?'

"'Same old thing,' one of 'em shrugs. 'Zamora laid us off again.'

"'Why?'

"'Hell! I don't know,' the guy says. 'Zamora claims because he fired us yesterday, it's like we're starting a new job today. So that means we gotta get new Referral Cards.'

"'That little son of a bitch!' I kinda mumble to myself, looking down. Then I take a big breath. 'Now look, I want you guys to stay here. I'll be right back.' I jump in the car and head for the ranch.

"About halfway there, I start running into the workers. They're all over the place, out in the road and along both sides of it, all walking back to Oxnard. As soon as I pull up, a bunch of 'em circle the car, all talking at once:

"'He can keep his damn tomatoes!'

"'Yeah, and his ninety cents an hour, too!'

"'No more of this going back and forth. We're through!'

"Right then this idea sorta hits, Fred (the second part of Plan XII): a way to let everyone in the state know what's going on. See, watching 'em all kinda marching I say to myself, Golly! If we could organize this thing right now and get 'em to turn around and march in the opposite direction, back to the ranch!

"But practically at that same second I think, Yeah, but who the hell would see 'em if we did it now? Nobody but Jones and the braceros. No, everybody's gotta know about this, and that'll all take time and publicity. Gotta think of some way to slow it down, get the workers to wait a while so the media can catch up with 'em. But how you gonna hold 'em, and where?

"That's when I get this other idea (the third part of Plan XII, Fred). The thing to do, I figure, we'll get 'em all back there at the F.P. trailer and have 'em wait right there. I check the Plan with some of the Employment Committee people I spot in the crowd, and they're all for it.

"'OK,' I tell the ones nearest the car. 'Get in.' Then I get up on the hood so the others can hear me: 'All the rest of you wait right here. We'll get some cars and pick you up right away.' I take off for the F.P. trailer.

"At the nearest phone, I get the word to James Flores at the office: 'Now look,' I tell him. 'Get all the publicity you can—press, radio, TV, the works. Then phone Carr and Crittendon what's happening. Oh yeah, and get ahold of a bunch of the housewives to bring some cars and fix something to eat for us. It's liable to be a long day.'"

Chapter 16

The March

"When I get back to the trailer with the first load, they all wanna know why we're stopping there. I tell 'em the first reasonable thing that comes to mind: 'We're gonna stay here because, well, we may get another job. Or plan something for tomorrow. The main thing is, we all gotta stick together.' Hell, I don't have any tried and true answer. All I know, we gotta hold 'em so we can march.

"See, Fred, this is what I meant a while ago about plans. I can't tell 'em the plan until we're all set to go. If you tell 'em, then you gotta march *right now*. If you think they're gonna sit around for two, three hours waiting for a buncha reporters and media guys, you're crazy! They'll just get out of the mood and walk away. Either that, or they'll all start marching right away, before we're ready to go.

"Before long, thanks God! here come the housewives and the cars James Flores sent to us, and we start taxiing the workers down to the F.P. trailer. It takes about an hour. All the time, I'm trying to think up some plan to make 'em stay there 'til we're ready to march. Well, the old 'plan producer' in my head seems to be out to lunch, so I tune back in to what the workers are talking about.

"They're all piled in around me there in the car, beefing about the lousy Referral Card trick Zamora pulled, when zingo! up pops Plan XIII: turn Zamora's trick against him! Get every damn worker to sign up for a Referral Card, even though most of 'em won't want to do it.

"In a way I hate it, Fred, because that's one of the things we've been fighting so hard against. But I can't think of anything else that'll take up a lotta time and hold 'em all together 'til we're ready. Besides, afterwards we can always tear 'em up or something.

"Anyway, when we get to the trailer, they all kinda crowd around me— men on one side, women on the other—wanting to know what's up. 'We're all gonna get Referral Cards,' I tell 'em.

"'Oh-o-o!' all of 'em groan. 'What for?'

"'Since when did any of you folks ever have any trouble figuring out what to do with a nice soft, square piece of paper?' I ask 'em.

"'That's all they're good for!' one of 'em sneers, and they all start laughing. Pretty quick, they're forming a line in front of the trailer.

"Well, by now, Fred, it's around noon and taco-time. The workers are building their little bonfires under the billboard by the road to heat up their tortillas. I'm just starting to drool at the smell when James Flores drives up beside me, loaded with sandwiches and coffee.

"'Qué suave.' I grab a sandwich. 'Did you get everything lined up?'

"'Sure, Cesar.' He's really excited. 'They're all on their way. The F.P. guys, Crittendon, the works.'

"'How about the publicity?'

"'Yeah, they're all coming too!' he grins. 'Even the TV truck, clear from L.A.!'

"While I'm chewing away, I start trying to think ahead about the March. First, there's the stuff I gotta warn the workers about. Like staying over to the side of the road. Not yelling or throwing stuff at passing cars. Spacing themselves so the line will look longer than it really is, you know.

"Then I have these worries about the Highway Patrol. I know that the second we start marching, the cops'll be right on our tails.

"But then, all at once, I get this kinda sick feeling that the workers might not go for the Plan, just wanna go home or something, and start walking away. So what? I tell myself. We'll have the March anyway—clear back to Oxnard! In a way, that would be just as good as marching out to Jones' because, in addition to all our other beefs, we'll have one about transportation: how they laid the workers off, and they had to walk all the way home!

"This is one of those 'alternate plans,' Fred, that the real hotshot organizers always have, you know, just in case the situation suddenly calls for a different approach. Of course, from what I've seen, those 'alternate plans' never really exist, except in the minds of 'Community Org' instructors who cradle-to-grave it on the campus. Or during a very brief period immediately before the particular action the plan leads to.

"Just then, here comes Villanueva with the Radio Remote Control Unit and a couple of reporters from the *Oxnard Courier*. James and I round up the 'old faithfuls' to get the word around among the workers that we're gonna march. I go over by the railroad tracks, where it's gonna start, and get up on top of my station wagon. When they've all swarmed around me, I give 'em those 'final instructions' I've been thinking about.

"I'm just finishing up when along comes this truckload of workers from some other ranch; it slams to a stop at the tracks. The second they spot us, they all start hanging over the sideboards wanting to know what's up. (And right here, Fred, is where the next carefully weighed and measured tactic of the overall battle strategy comes into play!)

"'Let's go!' I yell at 'em.

"'Where?' one of 'em yells back.

"'Jones Ranch,' I tell 'em. 'We're gonna march back there and get on TV and radio. Let everybody know how they're kicking the "locals" around. What do you say?'

"'Vámonos!' a bunch of 'em yell. 'Let's go!' They're crawling over the sides and tailgate when workers from two more trucks join them, and they all come scrambling out to get in line. That's when I give the starting signal, and the line moves out to the tune and rhythm of Pancho Villa's marching song, 'La Adelita.'

"For a while, we're the only ones on the road to the ranch. But all at once, the dust boils up and out of it comes the press, then the growers, then the 'brass' in State and Federal cars. The ten-car caravan of C.S.O. housewives that James sent out is just pulling in at the rear of the line when the first squad car skids up:

"'Attention! Attention!' comes the blatting voice through the speaker. 'I don't know what this is all about, but just keep it orderly, see? Otherwise we'll have to run the whole bunch of you in!' As the cop guns it up ahead to lead the line, one of the marchers yells:

"'Hey, we're bigshots.' He shoves his thumbs into his armpits. 'Police escort and everything.'

"Now it starts getting really trafficky. Five more cop cars slide up and cruise along beside us. About eight carloads of 'locals,' coming from work, get carried away and fall in behind the housewives. All this time, Villanueva is idling along the line with his remote-control outfit getting the workers to tell their story over the air.

"Too bad you missed it, Fred, it's really a ball! When we reach this little town El Rio—where I live, you know—all the people from all the stores start gathering on both sides of the road, waving and shouting: 'Hey, what's going on?' they wanna know. 'Where you going?'

"And all along the line, you can hear the workers: 'Jones Ranch!' they holler. 'He fired us and hired Nationals. Come on and help us, brothers and sisters, join the line!'

"This guy from CBS shows up. Rachel Guajardo walks up and hands him this piece of paper. 'Here's a prepared statement about our march,' she says. The CBS guy shoves the paper in his pocket and walks across to the line of workers, with Rachel trailing behind.

"That ticks off John. I tell him, 'The workers are getting in their two bits' worth, and that's all that matters.'

"'But hell, Cesar!' he kinda explodes. 'We should get out there, too.'

"'Are you worried, John?' I ask as we walk along.

"'It ain't that, Cesar,' he says, kinda lagging behind. 'It's just that we're doing all the work, and—Hey, Cesar!' I look around and he's pointing across the street: 'Now Eddie Perez is over there, too.'

"I only about half-hear him because of all this other stuff that's going through my head right then. Like, what are we gonna do when we get out to the ranch? How long can we hold the people? What's the final climax gonna be? Lotsa questions, you know, but no damned answers.

"I decide to bounce a few of 'em off old John. I even slow down to let him catch up with me, but there's no John! Looking back down the line, I finally spot him along with Rachel and Eddie, with the CBS guy and the mike!

"I can see the TV guy's not letting any of 'em take up much of his time. He just keeps talking to the workers in the line, trying to get them to say something into the mike. Instead of talking, though, they keep pointing in my direction. Pretty quick, he comes tearing up to me:

"'Hey, Chavez!' he kinda shouts, all outa breath, and asks all about the C.S.O. I make it as short as I can because I don't want to hog the show. When I finish, he says, 'Well, look, Mr. Chavez, why is it that a civic organization like the C.S.O. is interested in getting jobs for unemployed farm workers?'

"'Maybe it's just because we're interested in people,' I tell him. With that, the guy drops behind and John falls in beside me.

"About then, I can see Jones Ranch up ahead. There's a big 'reception committee' down there waiting for us—all the cops and brass and growers that passed us earlier. I hitch a ride to the gate with Villanueva. As the marchers come up, I get 'em to sit down among the eucalyptus trees that line the edge of the ranch.

"I've just finished with this when someone goes running by me like a bat outa hell. It's Eddie Perez running up the road that goes into the ranch. 'Véngase adentro!' he yells. 'Come on, you guys, we're going in!'

"'Wait a minute, Eddie.' I catch up with him. 'What are you trying to do?'

"'We're not gonna lie around out there on the road,' he yells. 'We're gonna march right out where the seedlings are. And sit down!'

"'We can't do that, Eddie,' I sorta plead with him. 'That's private—'

"'The hell we can't!' he yells, beckoning to the workers. 'Come on, you guys! You afraid or something?'

"Noticing a few of the workers are starting to mill around, I run over and get on top of Villanueva's truck where they can all see me:

"'Listen, everybody.' I raise my hands over my head. 'That's private property. You go in there, you're going to jail! You go to jail, C.S.O. can't help you. You're on your own!'

"The workers start to sit down again. 'Come on, you guys! We're going in!' Eddie yells.

"For a second nothing happens. The workers just stay where they are, looking at me and then at Eddie like there's a fight and they're waiting to see who's gonna win. Just then a cop busts out of the crowd and makes for Eddie:

"'Hey, you!' he yells. 'If you don't get your ass off that property, I'll run you in!'

"Eddie faces down the cop for a couple of seconds and then quiets down a little. Then the reporters and photographers start buttonholing Rachel and John, and there's flashbulbs all over the place.

"While all this is going on and I'm bumping around through the crowd, wondering what Plan XIV is going to be, I hear this reporter ask Chavira: 'Well, what's next?' So I know I'm right; something's gotta happen now. Something that'll sorta end the thing in a huge, dramatic climax. But what?

"Just then I recognize Zamora's voice: 'Naw,' he tells this reporter. 'They're just trying to stir up trouble with this marching business. They could all be working right now if they'd done like I told 'em and got their Referral Cards.'

"Soon as he says those words, Number One Ball of Plan XIV drops into the slot. I round up some of the 'old faithfuls' to see if we can't figure out some real exciting way of showing everybody what we think of those damn Cards:

"'Too bad it's out in public,' says Chavira. 'Otherwise we could all squat down, and—'

"'No,' Campos cuts in. 'But how about putting 'em in a hole with a burial ceremony and all?' As he's talking, I notice some of the workers warming themselves around a little bonfire, and zingo! the second ball drops in the slot.

"'How about that?' I point at the fire. None of 'em say anything. They just give me this look with their eyes and go over and start telling all the workers about Plan XIV.

"Well, you know how it is, Fred, with a bunch of reporters. Something sorta unexpected happens—like about the Cards—and right away they wanna see 'em and find out what we're gonna do with 'em, and why, and who and when, and all that stuff. When I see how big they're taking it and all, I figure maybe we oughta drag it out as long as we can. Make something really big out of it, you know. So what I do when I spot old man Campos coming up with all those cards stuffed in this hat of his, I start after him:

"No, no, no! Señor Campos!' I holler. 'Give the cards back to the workers. Each one has to burn his own.'

"So what happens, Fred, while Campos is handing back the cards to all those hundred workers, the reporters pick a couple of guys from each of the groups that are there, and ask 'em what they think about this card-burning idea. Well, right away Chavira and Flores tangle with some of the growers. This is great, Fred. It's the first time we've ever had what you might call a 'meeting' with the growers.

"But of course, the growers don't give a damn about the cards. They just come up with blasts against the march, because that's what's got 'em worried, you know.

"'These people don't wanna work,' one of 'em says. 'They just want to march.'

"The other grower says, 'If they wanna march, they should join the Army. Ha! Ha! Ha!'

"Then old Bates pops off: 'It's the law,' he says. 'Unless they have Referral Cards, we can't refer 'em; so they can't work.' (What he's actually saying, Fred, is that the F.P. guys can force the growers to hire the 'locals' if they really want to. And that is something we're never gonna let old Bates and Carter and Hayes forget!)

"By now, the workers are gathered around the fire, so I give the signal to go. Nothing happens for about fifteen seconds. Then Chavira steps out of the crowd and throws his card in the fire. As soon as it happens, everyone—even the growers—get real quiet. Actually, Fred, the way they all stand there with the firelight in their eyes, watching that card curl up and blacken, you'd think Chavira had thrown a hundred-dollar bill into the flames!

"It's amazing, Fred, the way the thing takes hold of the workers. In the beginning, each one comes up to the fire kinda slow. All of a sudden, though, the whole circle of workers seems to move at once, tightening up ten deep around the fire. It takes a long time to get the whole thing over, too, because the ones in front don't make room very fast for the ones behind. The reason for that, Fred, each one wants to stay up there next to the fire until his own card has burned clear up!

"This is when I start thinking what a lucky thing it is I had 'em burn their own. You see, Fred, they're doing what they marched out there to do—they're taking a crack at the enemy. Not only that, but each one, when he burns that card, is sort of committing himself never to go back for another one."

Chapter 17

Driving a Hard Bargain

"Next morning when I get to the office, the big room in front that old man Garcia has made into a rummage store is front-to-back, side-to-side, and floor-to-ceiling *workers*! They're perched on top of beat-up washing machines and Frigidaires and pianos with keys knocked out. They're packed into the double line of broken-down divans that form an aisle from the front door to my little office in back. They're crammed between long rows of used clothes racks that fill the rest of the room.

"I really don't know why they're there. We didn't tell 'em to come. Far as I know, they don't expect to go to work. Probably they're just there like I am, to see what's gonna happen next.

"Walking along the aisle toward the rear, I can tell from the bits and scraps of conversation that rise above the usual buzz that they're living yesterday's 'thriller' all over again:

"'. . . really fun!'

"'. . . scared at first, in front of all those people.'

"'. . . don't mind marching now at all.'

"'. . . saw me on TV last night!'

"'. . . talking in the mike. Is that how I really sound?'

"I notice a lot of 'em are looking at the morning *Courier*. Across the front page, there's a big picture of us marching along that dusty road. Some of the young guys are reading the story to the old-timers who don't know English.

"'Ay!' one of 'em points to the line of marchers. 'Is me!'

"'Mira!' Old man Campos puts his finger on the page. 'El Gigantón!' (It's John he's talking about, Fred, the 'Super Giant.')

"Mejia, next to him, gets his eyes down close to the paper: 'And who's the dwarf next to him? Oh, a thousand pardons, it's Cesar.'

"As I walk by, he and Campos and Chavira get up and join me. 'Hey, Cesar,' Chavira asks, 'is it really true we're gonna march again?' I wink at him and keep moving. Just as we get to the rear, Mejia pushes up:

"'Say, Cesar,' he says softly, 'did you see those Government cars this morning?'

"I swing around so fast I practically bump into him: 'What cars?'

"'The ones with the big "E" on the license,' he says.

"'Oh.' I go into the office and sit down. 'Probably cop cars.' For a second there, I'd hoped for something else.

"'We don't know.' Campos shakes his head. 'But we thought, seeing so many of 'em heading for the Assoc—'

"'The Association!' I cut in. 'Are you sure?' I keep looking from one to the other. After a second, they all start grinning.

"Just then, right on the other side of the little rail that separates the office from the rest of the room, this voice comes out kinda loud: 'Well, it's 7:30. Are we gonna go to work for Jones or ain't we?'

"I get up and stand by the rail, looking at the workers. Nobody answers the guy. They're just starting to gabble again when this woman sticks her head in the door:

"'Hey!' she yells. 'Here comes Jones' trucks!!'

"Fred, most mornings when the trucks show up, you start feeling real cheerful all of a sudden. You see 'em coming and you heave this big sigh of relief, like 'Thanks God! they're coming for 'em! They're gonna go to work,' you know. Then everybody practically knocks the door down going out. Me along with the rest.

"But this time, it's different. Oh, the good feeling begins all right. But right in the middle of it, all at once, I don't give a damn whether those trucks are there or not. In fact, I don't even want them there, if you want the truth. It's like Jones and Zamora and all of 'em think that the March and the burning and all didn't change a thing. Like they can just forget all those things and go right on from where they left off, driving us down that same old Rat Race over again.

"The workers must feel more or less the same, from the way they act. Nobody says anything. They just watch the trucks pull up, and then look over at me. About then, two guys and a woman slip out and get on a truck. But it's like those three just went to the can, or something. The workers just kinda half-watch 'em for a second, and then go on jabbering like nothing happened.

"Right then, three truck drivers come through the door and up to me: 'Well?' One of 'em raises his palms. 'When are the people leaving?'

"'People leaving?' I'm playing it real dumb, Fred. 'What do you mean?'

"'You know.' He sorta shifts around. 'We came for 'em.'

"'For what?' I ask him.

"'For work!' He gives me this 'what's-the-matter, you-nuts?' look.

"'For work?' I ask him. 'Where you from?'

"He turns away from me and slaps the air: 'You know where we're from. We're waiting for you guys.'

"'Well, OK.' I put my hands out toward the crowd. 'The people are here. Why don't you talk to them?'

"The driver turns to the workers: 'Well, let's go,' he says. Nobody moves. Then he gets this little smile and points through the window: 'Well, the trucks are out there. We're gonna work.'

"Some woman yells out: 'Who asked you to come for us?'

"'What makes you think we wanna work for Jones?' another one says.

"Most of 'em don't say anything. It's like they're gonna let all this horseshit sail by and just wait 'til the real thing happens. Finally, old Campos speaks up: 'You tell Jones if he wants us to go to work, he better come down here and talk to us.' Wow! Right on the head, Fred!

"The drivers have hardly pulled out when this feeling—sort of the opposite of the one I just had—hits me. You know, Fred, worrying about whether it was the right thing to do. Thinking, another day, another battle. Listening to how quiet the office is, and figuring the workers must be feeling the same way I do.

"Anyway, it's about twenty minutes later, and I'm back there with the 'old faithfuls' working on what to do next, when all at once I hear this big roar. Next thing I know, everybody's pushing up to the front looking outside to where these Government cars roll up. About six of 'em!

"'Hey, Chavez,' Chavira yells. 'It's Hayes!'

"When I hear that, all at once I know that the march and the way we've been playing it this morning is just exactly right! I start getting this real good feeling—confidence, I guess—and, at the same time, excitement! Like when you call some shot you're not real sure of and suddenly find out you're right.

"Well, I'm just sitting there in the back acting dumb, you know, when the door swings open and here comes about twenty State and Federal guys with Jones, Zamora, Crittendon and Hayes leading the pack. They come straight to the rear, and Hayes starts in on me:

"'Well,' he says, 'what gives?'

"'What gives, Mr. Hayes?' I'm playing it cool. 'Why, what do you mean?'

"'Well, uh—' He sorta jounces his head around and makes this wide gesture toward the workers. 'Why aren't these people working?'

"'I don't know, Mr. Hayes.' I sorta shrug. 'Maybe you better ask Mr. Jones and Mr. Zamora.'

"'But, uh—' He spreads his hands again. 'We've been waiting out there at the ranch for 'em.'

"I look straight at him: 'Whatever gave you the idea we were gonna go out there, Mr. Hayes?'

"'Well, I, uh—' His mouth sorta hangs open. 'Aren't you?'

"'No!'

"'But all you folks—' He looks around at the workers. 'You wanna work, don't you?'

"'Sure, we wanna work.' I keep looking at him.

"'Well, then—' He spreads his hands again. 'This is the job you've been trying to get. We're out there to see that you get it.'

"'No, Mr. Hayes,' I tell him. 'We've been out there for the last three days and couldn't get a job. What makes you think we'd go out there again today?'

"'Well, I don't understand this, Mr. Chavez.' He looks around at the other Government guys. 'I got a report last night that you folks were out there at Jones' place agitating for jobs, and now—'

"'Who gave you that report, Mr. Hayes? Your grower friends?'

"He sorta tosses his hands up: 'It was on the TV and the radio and newspapers all over the state. But that sort of activity won't get you anywhere.'

"'I'm not so sure of that, Mr. Hayes.' I wink over at the workers massing fifty deep outside the little rail. 'We've been trying to get jobs for a long time, but nobody except Crittendon ever helped us before. Now it looks like the whole State and Federal Government is in on the act.'

"Hayes' big, meaty face starts to burn: 'Regardless of that, Chavez, the main thing is we're here now and time's a-wasting. We better go to work. Hey, Zamora,' he calls to the Association manager, 'Get on the phone and call those trucks!' Zamora jumps toward the phone like he's been goosed.

"And you know, Fred, inside me I kinda jump, too. See, I never heard Turner or Bates, or even Crittendon, talk that way to Zamora before. The way Hayes said it, you'd think he was Zamora's boss or something.

"Then it pings into me. Why sure, there's the proof of what I was telling myself yesterday at the ranch: the F.P. is the boss, and Bates and Turner oughta be laying down the law to all the growers the way Hayes is doing it now with Zamora. The F.P.'s had the power all along; they're just so scared of the growers, or so lovey-dovey with 'em, they won't use it.

"Of course right now, when we've got 'em worried, it's different;

they'll use their power. Then, when the little emergency is over, they'll go right back to the good old days again. So the only way we can keep the F.P. cracking down on the growers is to scare the shit out of the F.P. ourselves, every time they let their grower-buddies break the law.

"Anyway, while Zamora's on the phone and Hayes is mickey-mousing it back and forth, the workers are getting a big kick out of it. All over the room, you can hear 'em talking in sort of almost-whispers:

"'. . . trucks are coming back!'

"'. . . think so?'

"'Sure they're coming back. And we're gonna play another trick on 'em!'

"In a little while, here come the trucks all right, Fred, but nobody moves.

"'OK,' says Hayes, looking around the room. 'The trucks are here.'

"'So?' I say.

"'So, let's get the people in 'em.' He makes a sort of scooping motion with his hands.

"'I can't get 'em in.' I shake my head.

"'Yeah, but time's a-wasting,' he says, sorta flaring up. 'You've been raising a lotta hell lately, Chavez. Now we're all set, so let's get to work.'

"'Not so fast, Mr. Hayes.' I push the front of my chair off the floor and kinda lean back. 'How do we know it isn't gonna be the same old thing?'

"He shoots his finger straight up over his head: 'I'll personally guarantee everybody gets a job!' Then he goes into this little speech to the workers about how they can always depend on him and all, you know. He's wasting his breath. Nobody pays any attention to him. Finally, I cut in:

"'OK, Mr. Hayes,' I tell him. 'Why don't we all sit down and talk it over?'

"'What are you talking about?' His eyes sorta bulge out like he can't hardly believe what he's hearing.

"'Sure,' I tell him. 'We've got a lotta grievances here, and the only ones who can do anything about 'em are you State people. So why don't we all get around the table here and see if we can't get 'em ironed out. If we make some progress, we'll go to work. If not, well—'

"'No, no, no!' He puts his hands over his eyes and shakes his head. 'You go to work now, and then we'll talk. It's getting late.'

"I just lean back there with my arms folded: 'Well, it's been going on like this for fifteen years or more, Mr. Hayes. I guess another forty-five minutes or an hour won't make much difference to anybody.'

"'No, no!' He raises his hands over his head and starts walking towards the door. 'You put 'em back to work and I'll meet you at the ranch.' He and the Government guys take off.

"Only Crittendon stays behind, looking at me with that little near-smile of his: 'What's up, Chavez?'

"'No,' I tell him. 'These people don't wanna work until we get this whole thing settled. Then we'll see.'

"'Good!' Crittendon nods and heads for the door. 'I'll see if I can get Hayes back here.'

"He's only been gone about fifteen minutes, when Carr calls. He comes on fast: 'Hayes tells me you guys won't work, Mr. Chavez. He wants to turn the braceros loose in Jones' seedlings. What's going on down there?'

"'I'm almost through giving Carr our side of it, when he breaks in again: 'All right, now, look. I'm gonna give Hayes orders to meet with you people at noon and get this whole damned thing squared away. Be sure and call me right after that meeting, Mr. Chavez. I want to know if you've been able to make any progress. OK?' He rings off.

"I give the workers the gist of that conversation and they select the 'old faithfuls' with Rachel, Eddie, John and me to represent them in dealing with Hayes.

"At 11:30 we're there in the Rec. Hall, having a little practice session before the brass arrives and the meeting gets underway.

"'Look,' I tell 'em. 'We all know we're not gonna get anywhere with this guy today or any day. The only way we're gonna get anywhere is to get rid of him!' I let that sink in for a second or two, and then I go on:

"'The best way to do that is to prove to Carr that Hayes won't work with us. So the second he starts trying to out-talk us and dodge the questions, like he did before, we get right up and walk outa here.

"'What we can't do is let Hayes ramble on for five or six hours. If we do, Carr'll probably figure Hayes is trying and maybe we're the ones that are being stubborn, and probably Hayes isn't such a bad guy after all. But if we knock it off fast and call Carr right away, then we'll beat Hayes to the punch.

"Well, Fred, I can tell they're not too crazy about this 'walking out' business. What they want is a nice long 'blow-off' session. Especially Rachel and Eddie and John. We're still arguing about it when here comes Hayes and the Government guys and Zamora and some of the growers.

"What Hayes is doing, Fred, he's trying to stack the meeting with all his pals and flunkies, figuring he'll snow us fast, get the workers back to the ranch, and then start bragging to Carr how good he is. So, to ram a little monkeywrench into that plan, we force him to get rid of all of 'em but Crittendon. Then I lay out the points for discussion: elimination of

Referral Cards, Gate Hiring, Pickup at the C.S.O. office, and an immediate wage survey.

"'If we make any progress on these points, Mr. Hayes,' I tell him, 'then we'll move to the question of whether the "locals" go back to Jones or not.'

"The meeting goes pretty good for about ten minutes, Fred. Then Hayes starts the usual: evading, bragging how he's the worker's friend. You know, the same old stuff, Fred. So I make my move.

"'Mr. Hayes,' I tell him, 'we've been through all this before, and I'm not about to sit through it all again. You negotiate with us on these four points. If you say no on all four, fine: that's the end of negotiations. If you say yes to three and no to one, well that's the end of negotiations too. But at least we got *somewhere*.

"'This is what I'm saying, Mr. Hayes: Either you give us a definite answer, or we're not gonna sit with you!'

"Watching him sit there practically smoking with indignation, Fred, I get the feeling that this time maybe we've got Hayes where we want him. Right then Rachel starts talking about the wage question, and the only way I can stop her is to tell her that the way things are, we can't even begin to get decent jobs unless we knock out those damned Referral Cards so the workers can go out and bargain directly with the individual growers. Instead of having to clear through the Association each time and get stopped cold. "But of course, Hayes isn't about to do anything about those Cards or anything else the workers want. So after he's dodged around on two of the four points and is just moving into the third, I cut in:

"'I don't know how the rest of you feel.' I look around the table. 'But to me, we're getting nowhere. Mr. Hayes has just made up his mind he's not gonna negotiate with us.' Right there, I start getting my papers together, Fred. 'I'm sorry, Mr. Hayes, but my time is valuable—and I know yours is, too. So I'm leaving!'

"As I head for the door, Hayes jumps up and puts his hand out toward me: 'Wait a minute, Mr. Chavez—' I just walk right down to the door and out.

"When I get outside of the Hall, suddenly I realize no one is following me. I look back in. Just like I figured! Fred. Oh, they're getting up and moving around a little, but you can tell they want to stay. Yeah, it's the same old business, thinking all their problems are gonna be solved just by having a meeting. Besides, they're getting a big charge out of pretending they've got Hayes cornered, even while they know they're not gonna get anything outa him. It's just sort of soothing to 'em, you know.

"I stay there till I see all of 'em moving toward the door. Then I go out and get in my car. I'm just pulling out when Hayes comes busting out of the midst of them and running toward me. I just drive on back to the office. When I get there, who's right behind me? You guessed it.

"Inside the office, Hayes sits down next to me at the desk, still trying to get me to return to the meeting. Finally, I tell him: 'Look, Mr. Hayes, I don't want to talk to you. You've been stalling for the last hour over there, and we know what to do with people like that. It's a lot different, you know, than when we met before.'

"'What do you mean?' he wants to know.

"'Just exactly that!' I tell him, reaching for the phone to call his boss. When Carr comes on, I can tell by his voice he's pretty worried:

"'Well, that was a short meeting,' he says, sorta coughing it out. 'How did it go?'

"'No progress,' I tell him.

"'Why?' he asks.

"'Don't ask me.' I look at Hayes. 'Why don't you ask your people?'

"'I want you to tell me,' he says.

"I just repeat it: 'No progress. That's all.'

"'Hey,' he kinda grunts. 'Who's there with you?'

"'Mr. Hayes is here,' I tell him.

"'Put him on!' he barks it out like he's pretty sore. I hand the phone to Hayes.

"Well, he goes on and on in a kind of groany voice: 'Well, I'm here, Mr. Carr, but the workers won't go back to work . . . . Oh, I've tried that, but Chavez won't negotiate. So what can I do? . . . Well, I know, Mr. Carr, but we've got the grower to consider too, you know . . . . Yes, but he's been after me all morning, you know . . . . Uh-huh, but don't forget, he's got to compete with the other seedling growers outside the Association, you know, and . . . . Well, as I told you before, the way I see it we have no alternative now but to let the Nationals pick the crop.'

"All at once, he hands me the phone. It's hot and sticky: 'Well, Mr. Chavez,' Carr chuckles, 'sounds to me like various people down there are pretty worried.'

"'Yeah,' I agree. 'But no progress.'

"Carr gives this quick laugh: 'I wouldn't be too sure about that, Mr. Chavez.' He laughs again and hangs up.

"A few minutes later, I'm walking Hayes to his car, and we pass a couple of workers leaning against the corner of the office.

"'Mira, es el hombre!' one of 'em says. 'Look, that's the guy!'

"'What guy?' the other one wants to know.

"'The real big one!' the first one answers in Spanish. 'He's the guy that can take every bracero out of this valley, just by snapping his fingers!'

"'Yeah?' the second guy says, with fake respect. 'Then why doesn't he snap 'em?' he chuckles.

"'You drive an awful hard bargain,' Hayes says, climbing into his car. 'I'm afraid you're heading for real trouble.'

"'Nothing new about that,' I tell him. 'But I sure wouldn't want to be in your shoes right now.'

"'Well, that's life,' he says and pulls away from the curb.

"That's the last time I ever saw him, Fred. The next I heard, he was heading up one of the largest growers' associations in California. Of course, when you come to think of it, it wasn't so much a matter of changing jobs as getting him on the right payroll, for a change!

"It's only a few minutes after he's gone when one of Jones' competitors, Tafoya, calls: 'Look, Chavez,' he says, 'can you get me four or five guys for the seedlings?'

"'Four or fi—!' The words jump out before I can stop 'em. This has never happened before, Fred; and my guard is clear down. Then I get hold of myself: 'Well, I don't know, Mr. Tafoya. Depends on what you're paying.'

"'Hell!' he sorta screeches at me. 'I'm paying same as Jones, ninety-five cents an hour.'

"'Yeah,' I string him along. 'That's one of the reasons they're not working for Jones. Not enough dough.'

"For a second, I don't hear anything but a kind of a grumble. 'Well,' he finally speaks up, 'tell you what I'll do, Chavez. You send me some good workers and I'll give 'em a buck an hour. But they gotta be good.'

"In the next little while, Fred, damned if two more calls don't come in from other growers for the same thing. It's just starting to get through to me that some kind of a real switch is going on, when here comes old Jones into the office looking sorta sheepish.

"'Hi, Chavez!' He slumps down in a chair. 'How many trucks you think I oughta send down here in the morning?'

"'I don't know, Mr. Jones.' I shake my head a little. 'I really don't. You saw what happened when you sent 'em down this morning.'

"'Yeah, but Christ, man!' He kinda starts out of the chair. 'I gotta get those plants pulled. If I don't get those orders out, I'm dead!'

"'What's the matter?' I bug him a little. 'Aren't you happy with your braceros?'

"'What are you talking about?' He looks up quick. 'I'm not using any

Nationals.'

"'How come?' I act real dumb.

"'Naw.' He gives this fast head-shake. 'Just causes too damned much commotion. You guys don't go out there today and then I take on Nationals. Then tomorrow, you guys change your mind and come out, and we've got the whole thing to go through all over again.'

"'Whata you care?' I play him along some more. 'As long as you get your seedlings pulled?'

"'No.' He scratches his head. 'It's just that the Assoc—'. He stops and starts again: 'Chavez, it's just that I figger the least trouble there is from now on, the better she'll be for all of us.'

"'Hmm.' I give him a little smile. 'Looks like somebody's taking the rap for somebody else, Mr. Jones.'

"'I don't know what you're talking about, Chavez.' He looks down and sorta jerks his head to one side. 'Thing is, I'm just small potatoes around here, you know. And I can't afford no more trouble because, well, for a lotta reasons.' He looks down at the floor for a second like he's thinking it over. Then his head comes up: 'Well, what do you say, Chavez? OK to send those trucks in the morning?'

"'Not for me to say, Mr. Jones.' I sorta dust off the top of my desk. 'That's up to the workers.'

"He looks at me kinda from under his eyebrows. 'Reckon they'll come?'

"'Who knows?' I sorta cramp my mouth a little before I give it to him: 'Tafoya's paying a buck, you know.'

"Wow! Fred, Jones' ears practically stand on end. 'He is?' He throws one leg over the other and kicks his foot out a couple of times. 'OK.' He nods real fast. 'I'll go a buck, too. Think that'll get 'em?'

"'I'll let you know after the meeting tonight,' I tell him. 'But if they do come back, I can tell you one thing for sure: If you ever pull any of that hiring-firing shit again, they won't just stay away for one day—they'll never come back! And you better tell your friend Zamora about that, too!'

"'A-a-a-h!' He slaps the air in front of him. 'You don't have to worry about that guy anymore. I'm handling the job myself from here on out.'

"'Well.' He gets up. 'Do your best for me, uh, Chavez?' At the door he slows and turns around: 'Say, by the way, Chavez, could I, uh, well, how's a feller go about joining this outfit?'

"'Oh, that's not hard, Mr. Jones,' I tell him. 'Only thing, we'll probably be fighting the growers for a long time to come, you know. And, of course pretty quick we'll be pushing a statewide minimum wage for farm workers. So if you join with us, I'm just wondering how all the growers who control the Association would take it. Without even mentioning all the growers in all the other associations up and down the state.

"Course that's not what worries me, Fred. What I'm thinking about is how the workers would practically stumble over each other quitting the C.S.O. if we ever let a grower join the outfit.

"'Yeah.' Jones sorta pulls at his chin. 'Sure, Chavez, sure.' He goes through the door and sticks his head back in: 'Be sure and call me right after your meeting, hear?' He takes off.

"Of course they all go back to work for him, Fred. Even though some of 'em have to argue like hell about it for a while. Some of 'em want to hold out till we win those points we were trying to negotiate with Hayes about. Others figure now that we've got Jones on the run, let's make him suffer a while before we give in. Then there are Rachel and Eddie and John, of course, out to raise a little hell.

"But none of their arguments hold up long. First place, we don't really have to worry much anymore about winning Gate Hiring and C.S.O. Office Pickup and Referral Cards: we're already starting to win 'em with the growers. On the matter of suffering, if we don't take those jobs with Jones, then he'll have to bring the braceros back, and then who'll suffer? And, of course, we can't strike because, unless we take the available jobs, we won't have anybody to strike against! So, however you look at it, there's only one way to go, and that's back to work."

Chapter 18

The Hour of Parting

"Well, Fred," Cesar said, "that sorta sums the whole thing up, I guess: how far the workers have come from where they were, along with the hell they had to put up with to get there.

"What next?" I asked.

"For one thing," he said, "we gotta keep the pressure on the F.P. to make sure we hold onto the gains we've made and keep making more. Also, now that we're opening up more jobs, we've got to go after a decent wage. Which means collective bargaining and the fight for contracts. In other words, a union.

"And sitting here tonight, Fred, I get this sort of a sad feeling like you get at 'la hora de despedida,' the hour of parting. Because that's just about where we are now, the point where C.S.O. bows out of the fight for jobs for the workers and lets the union carry on from here. As you know, that was our agreement with the United Packinghouse Workers at the very beginning. And Rachel and Eddie and the union brass in L.A. have been sorta hinting around for the switchover ever since that little sit-down strike we pulled at Jones Ranch. We can't put 'em off much longer.

"I hate to give it up, of course. It's as exciting as hell, and it's my— what's the word, Fred—my own 'domain.' I'm sorta the king, I guess. But besides that, now that I know the ropes a little, I'd like to push it one more year myself. Work out the rest of the kinks and get it set more solidly before we hand it over to the union.

"But that isn't all of it, Fred. What's really eating me, I guess, I'm just so damn scared the union people will take it and louse it up. Then we'll have it all to do again.

"But even that isn't all of it, is it, Cesar?"

"What do you mean?" he asked.

"Just that there's more to it than that," I said.

"Than what?" Of course I knew what he was doing. But I went for it anyway:

"Than Oxnard," I said, starting the car.

It must have been a full half-minute before he spoke again, very softly:
"Do you think I can do it?" he asked.

"I don't know, Cesar," I said, pulling away from the curb. "But if you
can't, I sure as hell don't know anyone who can!"

Then, from where he lay stretched out in his corner of the car came a soft
sighing, the sound of sleep.

Epilogue

Of course, the Packinghouse Workers Union didn't take advantage of all that work. But it didn't end there. Soon... Cesar moved to the barrio of East Los Angeles with his wife, Helen, and their now eight small children. Little Anthony had been born, and nearly didn't survive, during the Oxnard fight. Cesar worked registering tens of thousands more Mexican American voters in preparation for the 1960 presidential election (meeting with John Kennedy and his brother, Robert, who would later play a major role in the farm workers' movement).

But he couldn't keep living with himself without trying again to organize the farm workers with whom he had shared his life. Within three years after leaving Oxnard, he also left his beloved C.S.O. after the leadership of that organization would not commit itself wholeheartedly to farm worker organizing. Cesar gave up his C.S.O. paycheck (the only steady income he had in his life) and moved Helen and the eight kids to a dusty little farm town in the southern San Joaquin Valley named Delano.

Three years after that, in 1964, Congress voted to end the bracero program, although the growers never gave up efforts to revive some form of that hated plan. (It remains to be seen whether the farm labor program which is part of the 1986 Immigration Reform Law repeats the same abuses which marked its predecessor.)

In 1962, he founded the National Farm Workers Association (later to become the United Farm Workers of America) with ten members—he and his family—an old broken-down station wagon, and twelve hundred dollars in life savings which was soon gone. Helen worked in the vineyards to feed the family while Cesar babysat the younger children in the car as he drove to farm communities across the valley getting farm workers to join his infant union.

In September 1965, Cesar led his National Farm Workers Association (with twelve hundred member families) in a strike against Delano area grape growers begun by a largely Filipino union sponsored by the A.F.L.-C.I.O.

And then, he just walked into history.

But before the Grape Strike and Boycott, before the highly publicized marches and fasts, before the Kennedys, before the millions of people from all over the world who rallied behind his cause*—before all of that, there was just Cesar, with a single-minded doggedness that kept him trying no matter what the odds or how long it would take.

Thirty years later, he hasn't changed. Not one little bit.

---

* A 1975 nationwide Louis Harris survey revealed 17 million Americans boycotted grapes in support of the UFW. More recent polls indicate that Cesar Chavez and his movement continue to enjoy widespread public favor.

About the Author

Fred W. Ross was born in San Francisco in 1910, grew up in Los Angeles, and spent much of his life organizing in communities within both cities and in the scorching valleys in between.

During the Depression, Ross ran the federal migratory labor camp where John Steinbeck gathered material for *The Grapes of Wrath* and where Woody Guthrie sang his wonderful songs for the farm workers. When the government imprisoned Japanese Americans in concentration camps during World War II, Ross worked with the War Relocation Authority, helping thousands of camp residents to get out.

After the war, Ross organized eight Hispanic Unity Leagues in California's citrus belt, helping people battle segregation in schools, skating rinks, and movie theaters. In 1947, Chicago-based community organizer Saul Alinsky hired Fred Ross to help form the Community Service Organization (C.S.O.) in Los Angeles' eastside barrio. Under Ross' leadership, C.S.O. registered 50,000 new voters, elected the first Hispanic to the Los Angeles City Council, and won a major legal victory over brutality directed against Mexican Americans by Los Angeles police officers.

By 1952, Ross had expanded C.S.O. into Northern California, where he met and trained Cesar Chavez and persuaded his boss, Alinsky, to hire the unassuming young farm worker as a full-time C.S.O. organizer. Between them, the two men were responsible for the organization of 22 C.S.O. chapters; 18 still remained alive in the 1980's.

When Chavez quit C.S.O. to start his infant farm workers' union in the early 1960's, Ross worked for the National Presbyterian Church, organizing Yaqui Indians and Hispanics in Tempe, Arizona. In 1965-'66, he taught community organizing at the University of Syracuse. In 1966, Ross started training farm worker organizers for Chavez, helped lead United Farm Workers' field strikes, and trained the union's boycott organizers throughout the United States and Canada.

Most recently, in addition to his work with Chavez, Ross has trained organizers to stop the nuclear arms race and to halt the war in Central America. Ross is presently working part-time with his son, Fred Jr., in an anti-interventionist organization called Neighbor to Neighbor.